Migration and Populism in Bulgaria

Focussing on Bulgaria, this book addresses the key issues of migration and populism, which have grown to become dominant topics of debate within Europe and across the world over the last decade.

Ildiko Otova and Evelina Staykova trace the history of migration and populist discourses within Bulgaria from 1989 until the present day. The authors analyse how a lack of clear and coherent migration policies on migration over the years left Bulgaria unprepared for the 2015 European migrant crisis, thus leaving the door open for populist ideology to help shape public perceptions and narratives of migration as a menace and burden to society. Far from being confined to the extreme fringes of the political spectrum, Otova and Staykova reveal how populism has increasingly been co-opted by mainstream parties. This shift to the middle ground has led to what they claim to be a "normalisation" in populist rhetoric, giving legitimacy to attitudes towards migration as a threat to society, which they argue, in turn, renders constructive policymaking far more difficult.

Adopting an interdisciplinary approach, this book is an important tool for postgraduate students and researchers of Political Sciences, Migration Studies, European Studies and European History, as well as practitioners working in the field of international migration and asylum.

Ildiko Otova is a Guest Lecturer in European Migration Policies at Sofia University St. Kliment Ohridski, Bulgaria.

Evelina Staykova is an Assistant Professor in the Department of Political Sciences at New Bulgarian University in Sofia, Bulgaria.

Routledge Research on the Global Politics of Migration

For more information about this series, please visit: www.routledge.
com/Routledge-Research-on-the-Global-Politics-of-Migration/
book-series/GPM

Migration and Populism in Bulgaria

**Ildiko Otova and
Evelina Staykova**

Routledge
Taylor & Francis Group

LONDON AND NEW YORK

First published 2022
by Routledge
2 Park Square, Milton Park, Abingdon, Oxon OX14 4RN

and by Routledge
605 Third Avenue, New York, NY 10158

Routledge is an imprint of the Taylor & Francis Group, an informa business

British Library Cataloguing-in-Publication Data
A catalogue record for this book is available from the British Library

Library of Congress Cataloging-in-Publication Data
Names: Otova, Ildiko, author. | Staykova, Evelina, author.
Title: Migration and populism in Bulgaria / Ildiko Otova and
Evelina Staykova.
Description: Abingdon, Oxon ; New York, NY : Routledge, 2022. |
Series: Routledge research on the global politics of
migration | Includes bibliographical references and index.
Identifiers: LCCN 2021030449 (print) | LCCN 2021030450
(ebook) | ISBN 9780367752071 (hardback) | ISBN
9780367752088 (paperback) | ISBN 9781003161493 (ebook)
Subjects: LCSH: Bulgaria—Emigration and immigration—
Government policy. | Bulgaria—Emigration and
immigration—Political aspects. | Bulgaria—Emigration
and immigration—Public opinion. | Populism—Bulgaria. |
Bulgaria—Politics and government—1990–
Classification: LCC JV8303 .O76 2022 (print) | LCC JV8303
(ebook) | DDC 325.499—dc23
LC record available at https://lccn.loc.gov/2021030449
LC ebook record available at https://lccn.loc.gov/2021030450

ISBN: 978-0-367-75207-1 (hbk)
ISBN: 978-0-367-75208-8 (pbk)
ISBN: 978-1-003-16149-3 (ebk)

DOI: 10.4324/9781003161493

Typeset in Times New Roman
by codeMantra

Contents

Introduction

Migration and populism. Bulgarian specifics

Migration and populism have been among the major topics in European societies in recent years. Neither established Western-European democracies, nor the countries from Central and Eastern Europe have remained unaffected by these two phenomena. The present text examines the example of Bulgaria, which is interesting from the perspective of migration experience, but also because of the specific process of normalisation of populism in recent years.

It is not without a reason that we call migration "the watershed between two epochs". The closed Bulgarian society in the years of State socialism prior to 1989 recognises mobility and migration either as a privilege or as a trauma. There are very few chosen ones who had the right to travel, and those who managed to escape had to carry the stigma of non-returnees and the end of the regime was precipitated by the forced emigration of Bulgarian citizens of Turkish origin as a result of one of its most felonious acts – the so-called "Revival process". The few instances of immigration are also subject to political lines of logic. These processes have marked the migration profile of the country despite drastic differences in both the understanding and the policies in the area. It is no surprise that in the first years following the fall of the communist regime, migration and mobility have been perceived by Bulgarians as an expression of freedom. Even to this day, Bulgaria remains predominantly emigration country. These processes, however, are perceived in political talk, media interpretations and the public opinion mostly as a national catastrophe condemning the nation to extinction. The dynamic of emigration varies throughout post-1989 years. The factors can be grouped in two areas. Some are structural, among which one could cite the high unemployment rates, the risk of poverty and discrimination, the disintegration of main social systems after the political and economic changes. They are among the reasons of under-qualified and disqualifying labour migration, which can have

DOI: 10.4324/9781003161493-1

steady or circular character. The second area of factors is associated with the consummation of the "freedom to travel" in the 1990s; transformation of migration into mobility; especially after the factual EU membership achieved in 2007 and the lifting of travel restrictions and formation of a new citizenship beyond geographic locations.

Immigration for its part remained invisible to society. The few immigrants who have arrived to the country prior to 1989 are well integrated and thanks to their own efforts they have remained "invisible" to society. After 2007, the migration phenomenon becomes complicated in terms of both dynamics and processes. Thus, for example, there was a growing number of other member-state nationals with the parallel unfolding of the process of nationals arriving from the traditionally Bulgarian dispersion which – although strongly desired by politicians – were far from reaching substantial levels and a great deal of them simply cashed in on their origin through a Bulgarian passport which ensured easier access to the common European area. The connecting link between emigration and immigration are the returnees. This phenomenon has attracted the attention of society and media in the context of the financial crisis of 2009 and its most relevant manifestations are related to the pandemic crisis from the recent years. Not to be overlooked is also the significant role of the financial resources, which come into the Bulgarian economy from Bulgarians living abroad.

After 2015, the migration phenomenon was completely dominated by pressure from waves of the so-called "mixed migration", encountered by the EU, part of which passed through the territory of Bulgaria. Although there were moments of institutional "suffocation" for a short period of time, as we shall see in a while, the overcrowded accommodation centres were quickly emptied. The majority of those who had entered the country continued their way to Western Europe. To a certain degree, this type of migrational transit was facilitated by the political will or lack of a "humanitarian approach". The problem with asylum seekers in the country was highly politicised and they were strongly demonised in the media, which ultimately led to social tension. In the years after the beginning of the so-called migration crisis, the country allocated funds for the securitisation of the Bulgarian-Turkish border and, as rulers in Bulgaria have repeatedly stressed, they were working with their Turkish colleagues on quiet diplomatic channels to guarantee the security of the Bulgarian border, which is external border of the EU. The high point of this process took place in the beginning of 2020 when there were several thousand migrants on the Greek-Turkish border while at the Bulgarian there were none. The last months of emergency situation to the global has brought about the closure of borders for a couple of months but not to halting of migration. The Bulgarian case has repeatedly served as a conformation that what we are dealing with is a crisis of narratives rather than a crisis of numbers.

How to govern migration and integration when policies are absent – this is the question which to a great extent was valid for Bulgaria. If in the first years after 1989 migration was not recognised as a matter of political order, its politicisation after 2015 in the context of dominant populism created a situation where politics kill policies. The topic was derived into the status of policy through quick producing of numerous strategies and plans as a result of Bulgaria's accession to the EU. However, they failed to create steady public policies in the area of migration, but rather set the foundations of a securitarian, primordialist, and ethno-centric understanding of the phenomenon. The implications of the country's location on the Balkan Refugee Route not just solidified these readings, but also abruptly introduced migration into the political debate, where it is precisely through the discourse of politicians, media, and other public actors narratives of migration are created, which become mixed with the existing public attitudes and mutually intensify each other generating an overall environment of post truth, permanent sense of crisis, impossibility to produce policies and lack of actual governance of the processes. The periods of most distinctive presence of migration in the political discourse, however, coincide with those of freezing of policymaking in the area of migration, integration in particular, or of their failure, while the conversation is still missing – because the political actors do not seek to propose alternative visions, but to ensure who among them would give migration a more negative representation. The two leading trends can be summarised as erecting of walls – a fence along the border as regards the governance of the flows and halting the integration policies as regards the policies of incorporating migrants into society.

Populism, just like migration, has made its appearance in Bulgaria at a relatively late point when democracy could already be defined as consolidated, but it has settled permanently on the political scene. Although we may fundamentally accept the differentiation between populism and radical far-right, nationalism and nativism in the present book we have chosen to use the first term due to the broader scope of the concept. The process of normalisation of populism in the example of Bulgaria allows these characteristics to be detected with very few exceptions inside all populist and populism – "infected" parties. This becomes particularly visible through the example of migration. At the same time, we accept that this hypothesis would not be valid within different contexts, and we understand its limited character.

The text is structured into five chapters.

Chapter 1 exposes the reader to the specific migration experience of the country. Through the main dividing timeline – the transition from the closed communist regime to the open post-communist system – it conceptualises the specifics of the migration phenomenon in Bulgaria. The analysis is political-scientific and at the same time focussed on social attitudes and distances.

Chapter 2 focusses on post-1989 migration policies through several chronological and analytical inputs: first, the continuous absence of any policy whatsoever, not as some optional non-policy approach but as a lack of political understanding on migration in the initial years of democracy; in the second place, through the rapid development of numerous strategies and plans in the years of preparation for and active membership of the European Union, which do not, however, create sustainable public migration policies; and thirdly, in the years around the refugee crisis, which solidified the securitarian construal of migration in the political debate under dominant populist discourse. The refugee crisis evoked a completely new situation in which perceiving migration as a threat has become a steady symbolic universe. Apparently, the tendency for radicalisation of citizens was quickly instrumentalised by political actors. These two trends, however, act like interconnected vessels and mutually reinforce each other. Populist and extremist parties are most successful in exploiting the topic in resonance with societal attitudes, but they are not alone in enacting this type of mindset. Neither have any of the traditional political parties offered a viable alternative, rather on the contrary – they have reinforced the closed-border policy and intensified the anti-immigrant discourse. The methodology offers analysis of both documentation and policy programmes, as well as media analysis, including classic media and social networks.

The third chapter devotes particular attention to the refugee phenomenon. An overview of the great paradox of refugee policy in Bulgaria is presented by tracing the process of institutionalisation and the dynamics in the number of applications of protection seekers. Although it was asylum that became the earliest institutionalised form of migration, the state was totally unprepared for the 2012 situation, which placed it on the Balkan Refugee Route. Resulting from peaking numbers in asylum applications, new arrivals in the country were confronted by a situation of institutional collapse, political and media ostracism and mounting social tensions. Accommodation centres were unavailable, and in what were available the conditions were unacceptable. No working mechanisms for handling applications were in place, neither there were such as can ensure the bare minimum of standards to safeguard the protection of human rights. Despite ostensible normalisation of the situation in subsequent years, the reception system has failed to undergo significant changes on account of the crisis. Normalisation can be attributed to factors extraneous to the system, and the few changes to be affected came in response to the dominant securitarian reading and anti-immigrant sentiment. The analysis offers both a reading of the legislation and specific provisions in the field of international protection and the system of reception, as well as the actual situation based on field research.

Chapter 4 theorises the topic of populism, not just by presenting classical definitions of this phenomenon, but also by introducing a specific reading for the Bulgarian context. Some analysts count on the inclusion of far-right parties in governments as a tendency in view of their domestication, but in fact what happens is a process of classic parties coming near extreme ideologies. Tracing the development of populist parties on the Bulgarian political scene and, mainly, analysing the degree to which classic parties approximate the extremist discourse in the years of the refugee crisis, prompts a crucial question – whether what happened during the migratory pressure was not so much a migration crisis rather than an overall crisis in the political and social processes.

The last chapter is devoted to solidarity coming in response to dominant populism. In view of what has been said so far, it is hardly a surprise that, paradoxically, although Bulgaria has practically harmonised its asylum legislation with that of the European Union, one can hardly speak of Europeanisation of the migration topic, but rather about its nationalisation and closure in the local debate. Missing, for example, is a substantive discussion on quota redistribution or a national debate on the revision of the Common European Asylum System. On the one hand, the role of the European institutions and international organisations is examined, also providing a critical view of the situation, wherein they tangibly fill in for lacking policies, but at the same time engender a false sense of a functioning system. On the other hand, the role of the non-government sector and civic activism is considered as a small but powerful counterbalance to the status quo. In addition to the theoretical treatment of the topic of civic activity, the text utilises a wealth of empirical material.

"The long summer of migration" has drastically affected European societies. Migration, which can be capitalised upon as a demographic, intellectual, and cultural potential, was instrumentalised in a demonising fashion by the populist wave, which has swept over Europe – as a menace and as a burden. Bulgarian specifics provide an interesting field, affording opportunities for wider theoretical interpretations. The short migration history and the ongoing transit character of the migratory flows have clearly outlined the tendency of populist discourses to engender societal notions transcending the data-based realities. The construction of symbolic universes by a wide range of political actors has been used to substitute real problems of society by way of conjuring up enemies – whether asylum-seeking migrants, traditional minorities, sexual minorities, or even international documents such as the Istanbul Convention. These Bulgarian lessons provide a good reference point for analysis of both European and global tendencies.

1 (Re)discovering migration – the post-1989 migration profile of Bulgaria

Bulgaria continues to be a state affected mostly by emigration, but neither politicians and statesmen, nor society have managed to comprehend and analyse the factors, which effected the departure of so many nationals out of the country despite the dramatic way they perceive and articulate the phenomenon in terms of a serious demographic problem verging on a national catastrophe. Even if there is still some fragile dynamics of returning emigrants, resulting, for instance, from the Covid-19 pandemic, it happens as a conjuncture of factors, without understanding the possibility and the necessity of governing the process. Substantial levels of economic emigration and the social and economic context in conjunction with the geographic location make the country a point of origin and a transit territory for the darkest phenomenon of migration – human trafficking. Another trend of recent years which should not be overlooked is the tendency of transnational civil activity developing within certain groups of emigrants.

On the other hand, the post-1989 changes, followed by the 2007 accession to the EU, have brought the country nearer to normalisation of immigration in terms of causes and forms, although in purely statistical terms it has remained at very low levels. Economic immigration, along with asylum granting, is some of the forms of migration rediscovered by Bulgaria in the course of the democratic changes. Immigration in the country is of complex and mixed nature. EU citizens, third-country nationals, old and new migration communities comprise a small but varied local immigration panorama. International commitments and the fact that the country manages the external border of the EU account for the flows of asylum seekers streaming to Bulgaria, especially after its location was found to coincide with the Balkan Refugee Route. Of particular importance to the understanding of Bulgaria's case is the highly politicised treatment of the migration topic in the

DOI: 10.4324/9781003161493-2

years after 2013, which found expression in a traumatic experiencing of emigration and dramatic discovery of immigration.

The first part of this chapter presents the migration panorama of Bulgaria, and the second provides a closer focus on the interpretations, chiefly of emigration processes. This is a political-science analysis, but it will also focus on some social attitudes and distances.

Migration as a watershed of two epochs

Any analysis of migration processes in Bulgaria needs to take into consideration the communist past of the country. The reason for this, above and beyond any political connotations, is the fundamental difference in migration nature and the way it is managed before and after the changes (Staykova, 2013). Comprehension of current processes would be impossible unless they were viewed within the context of this transition between two epochs, for which migration acts as a watershed. The reason is that a substantial part of the contemporary migration phenomenon is related to realities inherited from former migratory processes. Thus, for example, old migrant communities, who arrived to Bulgaria during the communist period on account of ideological propinquity or the so-called "fraternal agreements", are seen today to attract fresh economic migration, which utilises established networks and a successful integration of the forerunners into the recipient society. The very outset of the transition was marked by a massive migration wave, and the subsequent opening of borders was definitive for the migration profile of the country as well as crucial in the formation of certain societal attitudes.

Going back to the period before 1989, the analysis should take into consideration the fact that even though communism as ideology may be perceived as a global and open movement (Ditchev, 2003), it has bred some exceptionally closed societies, which monitored tightly who crossed outside the county's borders and who entered its territory. Nationals were expected to be static rather than mobile. Movement and mobility even within the state's own national territory represented a controlled process and not a matter of personal freedom or wish. To a much greater extent, this applied to trans-border traffic. In view of the above, it is not a surprise that both immigration and emigration have eminently found a place within the political logical models (Krasteva, 2014b).

Immigration in Communist Bulgaria, although severely restricted, seemed less problematic than emigration, insofar it did not directly affect the liberties of Bulgarian nationals themselves. Explicably, the most numerous group was represented by immigrants from the Soviet

Union, in their best part women who came to Bulgaria as wives of local nationals. Despite expectations of both Sofia and Moscow regimes that the process would in effect lead to "sovietization" of the country (Krasteva, 2014b), it has largely remained an instance of "sentimental migration" (Atanasova, 2005).

Several other groups can be cited as examples, with more ideological explanations to be sought behind them (Krasteva, 2005). The group of political refugees is not numerous, involving mostly people of leftist persuasions, with the immigrants from Greece being a specific example. Greek political migrants come in two identities – guerrilla fighters and civilians running from the war (1940–1944), as well as children, evacuated by the Communist Party towards some socialist-bloc countries (Kokinu, 2012). A small part of this group has remained in Bulgaria.

The second group comprises students from "fraternal communist countries", or the so-called "Third World", who have received scholarships for study in Bulgarian universities. Bulgaria granted government scholarships to young Africans by virtue of interstate arrangements. The only research made so far on migration of Africans into the country (Kamenova, 2005) states that the period after the 1970s saw an average of about 360 students come to the country, and by the end of the period educational stipends began to be granted also by other structures, such as the Fatherland Front, the Central Cooperative Union, the Academy for Public Sciences and Social Management, the Committee for Solidarity with the Peoples of Asia and Africa. Immigration from the Middle East was more numerous and followed the same logic of relations with "fraternal countries" – among them Syria, Lebanon, the Palestinian Territories, Iraq, Jordan, Iran, Afghanistan (Krasteva, 2014b). Very few of the African students stayed in Bulgaria, and those from the other group have remained mainly because they had contracted marriages, some of them eventually returning to their native countries after 1989.

There is an example of economic migration with inherent ideological aspect represented by the expatriate workforce from Vietnam, employed primarily in the field of construction works (Krasteva, 2014b) upon signing the labour pact between the two countries in the late 1970s (Mitseva, 2005). It is noteworthy that by the end of the regime and in the first years after 1989, the Vietnamese were "expelled" from the country (Apostolova, 2017).

Emigration at the time was little and very limited. Exit visa system with its exceptionally selective and restrictive accessibility (Krasteva, 2014b) represented the most distinctive manifestation of migration policing in Communist Bulgaria. Exceptions were few. A "naturally chosen" destination was the Soviet Union – for purposes of education and employment. At the end of the 1970s, pursuant to agreements with other socialist states, as well as some North African regimes, few "elect" were able to travel and work to these foreign locations as experts in the field of medicine or engineering sciences, or as workforce for a specified employment term (Krasteva, 2014b).

Emigration from Communist Bulgaria, however, has lingered permanently in the collective memory precisely for its selectivity and for its status of discriminately accorded privilege. Its traumatic images are no less vivid. The communist regime coined the term "nevuzvrashtenets" (a "defector", a "non-returnee"). Even legislation from the 1948 to 1989 period penalised various forms of unauthorised departure from the country – initially by divesture of citizenship and expropriation of the entire property, later by a ten-year term of imprisonment and a forfeiture of 50,000 leva, and after 1953 it began to treat it as a "treason of the motherland" and to punish it with death. The period in the 1970s following the events in Czechoslovakia was marked by an upsurge of new measures designed to combat emigration (Kiryakov, 2011). As a result, Bulgarian citizens moved abroad mostly as refugees.[1] About 20,000 Bulgarians left the country between the end of the 1950s and 1989. By contrast with other countries of Central and Eastern Europe, which saw dramatic outflows of refugees, figures for Bulgaria indicate that numbers remained stable over time: about 370 persons annually (Sultanova, 2006).

Another example of emigration during the period of the communist regime was of forcible character. At the end of the 1980s authorities commenced the so-called "Revival Process".[2] During a massive exodus euphemistically labelled "Grand Excursion" in the spring of 1989, over 350,000 Bulgarian nationals of Turkish origin were forced to leave the country (Maeva, 2006). The collapse of the regime in November of the same year was marked and – in the opinion of some – accelerated by these events and the substantial wave of forced ethnic migration.[3]

The democratic reforms in Bulgaria marked a radical change in the country's migration picture. One of the earliest changes which followed the collapse of the communist regime was related precisely to the freedom of movement – the abolition of the exit visa system.[4] Freedom of movement became one of the first and most eagerly consumed freedoms (Krasteva, 2016). In the following years, the logic of politics would get mixed with purely economic considerations (Hristova-Balkanska, 2012, p. 93).

Due to economic transformation taking place at the time, attended by soaring inflation, unemployment, and political instability, many people decided to emigrate in search of better personal opportunities

(Mancheva and Troeva, 2011; Staykova, 2013; Petrunov, 2014). Krasteva (2019) describes the situation, on the one hand, as a loss of demographic, social, educational, and democratic capital, but, on the other hand – as a way to contribute to the country's development through substantial money amounts being remitted back home. The economic and political chaos of that period also engendered an environment conducive to the emergence of organised criminal groups, seeking to cash-in on people's desire to find employment and to organise human trafficking networks (Petrunov, 2014). This tendency of emigration of both high-skilled and low-skilled workers was only intensified by the accession of Bulgaria to the European Union in 2007 (Mancheva and Troeva, 2011). Ivan Krastev and Stephen Holmes remind us that nevertheless

> we should keep in mind not only the significant difference in standards of living between West and East and the logistical ease of the move but also one of the least discussed legacies of communism, namely the memory of how bureaucratically difficult it had been to change one's place of residence.
>
> (Krastev and Holmes, 2019, p. 56)

In this sense, the symbolic impact of mobility and migration is of no less consequence and exerts no smaller influence on societal attitudes.

The total number of Bulgarian nationals living abroad, by various estimates, vacillates between a little over 1 million and nearly 2 million and a half. However, in the last three decades, the data indicate a tendency of significant decrease in the number of people leaving Bulgaria. The average net annual rate of migration, indicating 66,000 departures in the late 1980s, decreased to about 27,000 people in the 1990s and to 17,000 people between 2001 and 2011 (Angelov and Lessenski, 2017a). Eurostat data indicate that between 2013 and 2019 the number of Bulgarians leaving the country registers a gradual increase, with the number doubling over a five-year period – from 16,000 in 2013 to 31,000 in 2018 (Eurostat, 2020).

The largest number of people left Bulgaria when there were visa restrictions, when the country was in the negative Schengen list and there were considerable impediments to labour migration. Conversely, the last decade saw a decrease in net migration despite EU membership, the visa-free regime with over 150 countries around the world and the freedom of movement, work, and residency within the EU (Angelov and Lessenski, 2017a). In 2018 about 13.3% of the working age population of the country (20–64 years) is mobile. In the second part of this chapter, we shall return to these numbers and mostly to their interpretations. In the next paragraphs we shall focus on the destinations and the profile of the emigrants.

What is relatively clear is that a large portion of Bulgarian expatriates – around 900,000 – reside in Europe. Germany is a powerful attraction pole for both low-skilled and high-skilled workforce (Krasteva, 2019). It is the most desirable country for migration, with about 340,000 Bulgarians living there by 2019. Mediterranean countries, such as Greece and Italy, are also very attractive to Bulgarian emigrants. A traditional country for Bulgarian guest workers, such as Spain, reports a serious outflow since 2009 (the peak year for Bulgarians living in the country – about 151,000 people). So far, the number of Bulgarians has decreased by almost 29,000 people. This is the result of the extended recession of the Spanish economy and the collapse of the construction sector, which used to employ a large proportion of Bulgarian citizens. Some of them returned to Bulgaria and others moved on to other European countries (Ivanova et al., 2019). On the other hand, Belgium is also a top employment destination among Bulgarians, with a total number of 37,000 residents in 2019. Most of them are employed in the construction, hotel and restaurant sector and cosmetic services according to the observations of our compatriots (Ivanova et al., 2019). Bulgarian nationals in the UK have also registered a decrease in numbers, but in this case the decrease was due to the Brexit (Capital, 2019b). The classic immigration countries – the US and Canada – continue to act as magnets even today.

Concerning gender distribution, in the case of emigration, men tend to outnumber women throughout the period 2010–2017, but numbers for both sexes were almost equal for some years – this for 2013, of all Bulgarian emigrants 9,841 were men and 9,837 were women. Bulgaria's case illustrates a global trend towards feminisation of migrations in both quantitative and qualitative terms: regarding migration flows, where numbers are growing of female migrants and have become nearly equal to those of the males; and regarding agency and authorship of the migration project. Some women accompany their husbands, parents, or relatives, but many women plan and realise their migration project on their own (Krasteva, 2019).

For the purposes of the present analysis and without any claim to exhaustiveness,[5] a different approach shall be employed, structuring two groups of migration-enabling causes:

- structural factors, such as high unemployment rates, risk of poverty and dissolution of the principal social systems in the wake of the 1989 political and economic changes, which have become the underlying reason for huge waves of low-qualified or de-qualifying

labour migration, which may have a stable or circular character, with a special accent on the migration of the Bulgarian Roma people, and in which human traffic has emerged as the final form;
- factors associated with the "freedom to travel" in the 1990s; transformation of migration into mobility; especially after the factual EU membership and the abolition of the restrictions on travel and formation of a new citizenship beyond geographic locations.

Undoubtedly, the most numerous group is the group of labour migrants. In this sense, talking about emigration, it is important to note the huge dependency of Bulgaria on the money allowances emigrants send back home. According to data of the World Bank for 2018, the share of these remittances in the Gross Domestic Product amounts to 3.8%.[6]

For a country like Bulgaria, one should bear in mind that the end consumption is a basic driver of growth. Money from emigrants flows precisely there, with the best part of this monetary stream designated for covering current expenses, healthcare, education, and redemption of loans. Thousands of families depend on the support from relatives abroad to pay bills and to subsist. Nevertheless, there is a positive detail to be noted that many small family businesses have also engaged in some economic activity because of the financial of a relative abroad. During the last ten years the flows of emigrant money managed to regain their pre-crisis levels from before 2008. In 2020, however, they were again significantly reduced due to the pandemic.[7]

As demonstrated by the world-wide practice, migrants residing in a country for a shorter period make more frequent and in larger sums money transfers than long-term settlers and long-term sojourners, meaning that the intensity of money remittances is not so much associated just with the support of relatives, than with the plans of the migrants to return to their own country. This also makes migrant savings a potential resource for stimulating the development of the countries with substantial migration. The case of emigrant waves coming from Bulgaria provides an eloquent support of this thesis. The largest emigrant wave from the end of the 1980s, which essentially had expatriation character, did not lead to a substantial increase in remittances, while current short-term labour migration, considerably smaller in scope, is surprising for the enormous amounts of money remittances it has entailed (Bobeva, 2004).

The money remittances, as has become clear from the afore said, though coming in different amounts and intended for different purposes, end up in the country after being sent by emigrants, whose reasons to leave Bulgaria can be outlined in the two groups of factors, which we have pointed out.

Against this background, Western-European societies regard Bulgarians as being in the category of "poverty migration", like most migrants originating from Eastern Europe. In discourse situations, where such interpretations are articulated, Bulgarians can be described as migrants who supposedly 'abuse' the already stretched welfare systems of the Western states. The migrants do so by applying for social benefits, while simultaneously getting engaged in irregular labour. The 'abuser' is presented in the image of a low-skilled and impoverished migrant defrauding the affluent Western state by milking social benefits without contributing by way of taxes and regular employment (Deneva, 2014). Within Bulgarian society itself, it is the people of Romani origin that become the subject of such discourses. The collective vilifying depiction of Bulgarian nationals of Romani origin is projected by the media and the politicians and has been a steady constant in the years after 1989, which is impossible to overcome even through statistics, data, or good examples (Deneva, 2014). Romani are among the people who took the brunt of the economic upheavals of the 1990s and the high rates of unemployment (Deneva, 2014, p. 48).[8] In this sense, there is nothing surprising in the high rates of emigration – most often circular and temporary – within this community. Like many other aspects of the migration phenomenon, mobility and emigration among Bulgarian Romani people is unfortunately not extensively examined in Bulgarian academic circles. An interesting research by Neda Deneva is based on field work carried out in several cities in Bulgaria and Europe. In her estimate:

> the Roma migration profile neatly fits and fuels the stereotype of the "poverty migrant". Some work irregularly in short-term jobs ranging from domestic services, construction work, road repairs, and factory work – in barely legal arrangements. Others find a source of income in regularized forms of begging, selling street newspapers or playing music in designated street spots. In addition, most of them rely heavily on various forms of social benefits, sometimes participating in fraud schemes.
>
> (Deneva, 2014, p. 50)

A similar assessment can be found in a research titled *The Faces of Roma migration in the EU*, conducted in the period 2015–2017. An interesting highlight, however, is that Roma migration is a social process, in which they accumulate knowledge and skills (Mineva, 2018). This understanding of migration as a social capital has its validity and could be of crucial importance mostly in the development of adequate policies with respect to diversity governance.

A specific figure, associated with the Bulgarian migration phenomenon after the changes and representing the worst example of peacetime forced migration, is the human-trafficking victim (Krasteva, 2014a). Bulgaria is mainly a country of origin of human trafficking and to a lesser degree a transit country. Victims of human trafficking for Bulgaria number 400–550 annually. The main countries of destination are EU Member States such as Greece, the Czech Republic, France, Sweden or Switzerland and Norway. The most prevalent form of trafficking is the one run with the purpose of sexual exploitation, followed by labour trafficking exploitation. Most victims are female (European Commission, 2018b). The report of the US Department of state for 2019 shows that traffickers exploit Bulgarian women and children in sex trafficking – (Office to Monitor and Combat Trafficking in Persons, 2021). Conspicuous trends include the steady increase of registered victims trafficked for the purposes of labour exploitation, also among women; targeting of mentally disadvantaged people by traffickers, the relative decrease in the use of violence by the criminals in preference to more sophisticated methods such as deception and emotional dependency and increasing use of internet and social networks by traffickers for recruitment purposes (European Commission, 2018). Social and economic factors are among the main reasons for these high levels. There are some other factors to be emphasised as well, relating mainly to the lack of qualification capacities in legislative authorities and the high corruption rates. This gives the US State Department a reason to conclude: "The overall evaluation is that the Government of Bulgaria does not fully meet the minimum standards for the elimination of trafficking but is making significant efforts to do so" (Office to Monitor and Combat Trafficking in Persons, 2021).

The migration of highly qualified experts, as well as educational migration, emerges on the diametrically opposite extremity. It is precisely the type of migration responsible to the greatest extent for the formation of a new type of citizenship, which goes beyond geographic locations. Contemporary processes reveal that mobility and civil engagement often go hand in hand. Mobility does not reduce the vitality of citizenship; on the contrary, it makes citizenship more creative and innovative. Traditionally, the migrant dispersion is seen as solidary with the commonwealth – in terms of state, language, and family, but:

> The social networks and the protests have become the demiurge of a new, digital diaspora, whose connections are built by a

trans-border, active and socially engaged citizenship. Solidarity is no longer with the state, but with the citizens against the irresponsible and corrupt state.

(Krasteva, 2013a, p. 10)

The classic phrase from the early years of the transition that Bulgarians vote "with their feet", is becoming less and less true. Leaving the country is not an escape from civil commitment – this is demonstrated by the numerous activities held in solidarity with the Sofia protests both in 2014 and in subsequent years.[9] There was considerable participation on the part of mobile Bulgarians, returning to the country for the 2020 summer protests during the Covid-19 pandemic.[10] This context should also comprise the numerous initiatives and attempts of expatiate Bulgarians to accede to the actual right of participation in political life through inaugurating polling sections and introducing mail voting or remote electronic vote.

To summarise Bulgaria's migration phenomenon, it is dynamic and variable, flexible and fluid – it readily passes from one form to another; what is of essential importance, however, is that it affects the mobile and immobile Bulgarians alike.[11]

On the background of emigration, immigration appears insignificant and radically different from the classical phenomenon inherent to Western Europe (Krasteva, 2013; Angelov, 2017). The total number of immigrants does not exceed 2% of the populace (OECD, 2019). Researches show immigrants to be well-integrated in terms of labour market participation, linguistic, cultural, and social integration (Krasteva, 2019). This renders the phenomenon equally "invisible" to politicians who only with difficulty and too late derive it into a public policy, and to citizens who, for the course of the two decades following the democratic changes, have never articulated it as a problem and had no reason to do so.

One can get an idea about the dynamics of the migration phenomenon from the statistical information provided by the National Statistical Institute (NSI). The NIS data are broken down by gender, age, and nationality. The analysis of this indicator has its limitations. On the one hand, the NIS studies the process through the prism of demographic statistics. This implies that the study focusses on the number of emigrants and immigrants, but it fails to employ a detailed analysis of their profile and motivation.

Data suggest that in the last ten years, between 2010 and 2019, the number of individuals who have declared before the administrative authorities a change of their current address from abroad into the country, has increased by ten times. A peculiar feature of the statistics, however, is that in the total number of permanent settlers in the country, the NIS also includes individuals who were born in the country and/or have Bulgarian citizenship (Figure 1.1).

This detailed scrutiny of the data brings out an important migration phenomenon – of those who are returning. The very fact that NIS, in its own data, has failed to distinguish homecoming Bulgarian nationals from immigrants is sufficiently suggestive of the state's attitude to the policies in these two areas. A slight digression should be made to address the topic of the repatriates, as it is of interest for the overall analysis. As it turns out, a substantial portion of the people who have entered the country in the recent years comprises precisely Bulgarian nationals returning to their native country. This process became observable as a more consistent trend after 2013, when over ten thousand Bulgaria-born people began to return annually to the country. The number was twice greater than 2013 figures when returning Bulgarian nationals numbered 4,771. This influx, although smaller than the outgoing migration flow, indicates the beginning of a process of reverse migration and a trend of return to Bulgaria. Curiously enough, this tendency was dynamised by the Covid crisis, and by an expert appraisal over 500 thousand Bulgarian nationals are estimated to have returned to the country, which is a huge number for a country with 7 million population. According to a recent

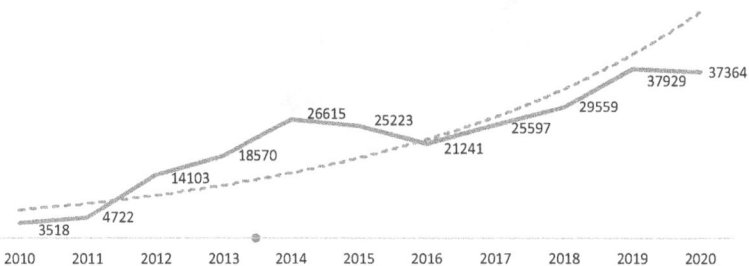

Figure 1.1 Outgoing migration-total for the country*.

* The statistics includes only those individuals who have declared before the administrative authorities a change in the address of their permanent residence (place of abode) from abroad into the country.

Source: Authors after data from the NIS.

research about two-thirds of the Bulgarians who have returned are making plans to migrate again (Georgiev, 2020). It should be noted, however, that this research was conducted at the end of 2020, when there was still no awareness as to the long-term duration of the crisis. Although there was no subsequent research, it is important to note that at this stage there is no programme to support the returnees. As demonstrated by both theory and practice, reintegration into society often requires effort and support. This ascertainment is of particular interest because immigration in Bulgaria is experienced in a particularly traumatic way and attracting emigrants back to the country is not just a goal statement, laid down in strategic documents, as we shall see in the next part, but also tend to be frequently used as a romantic refrain by politicians across the spectrum which, however, has yet to crystallise into a policy.

And to reprise the topic immigration in Bulgaria, there is another important observation, highlighted in the breakdown of statistical data gleaned by the NSI. It seems that Bulgaria is of greater interest to migrants originating from countries outside the EU (Figure 1.2).

The dynamics of migration is also implied by the total number of third-country nationals, who have obtained permission for extended or permanent residence in the country. Data indicate that the number of issued permits has increased three times over five years: from 13,670 in 2015 to 45,236 in 2019 (Figure 1.3).

For 2017, Turkey, Russia, and Syria were the top three newcomer nationalities. Among the top 15 countries of origin, Syria registered

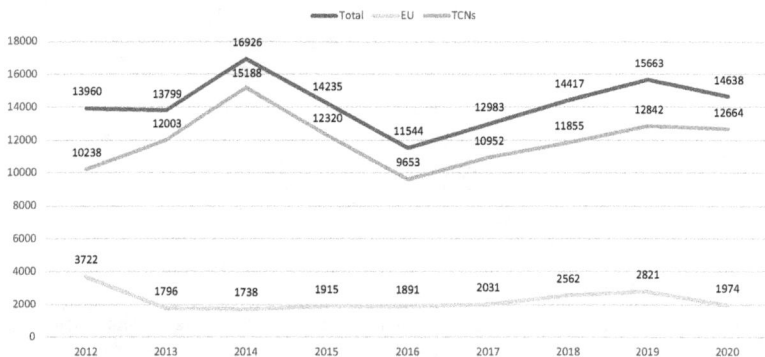

Figure 1.2 Immigrants by place of birth.
Source: Authors after data from the NIS.

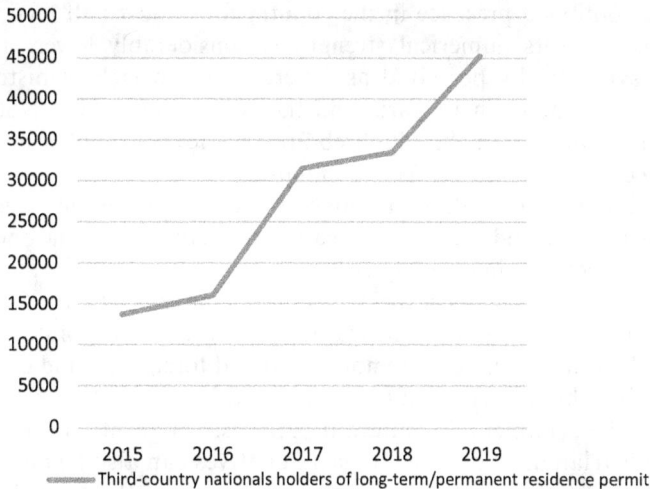

Figure 1.3 Third-country nationals holders of long-term/permanent residence permit.

Source: Authors after data from the NIS.

the strongest increase and Russia the largest decrease. Of immigrants who have obtained residence permit for a term longer than 12 months in Bulgaria, 11.3% are labour migrants, 23.5% are family members, 7.3% came for education reasons, and 57.9% represent other migrants (OECD, 2019) (Figure 1.4).

As of 2011, Anna Krasteva described immigration to Bulgaria after 1989 in five main aspects:

• the largest group with the longest standing tradition comprises immigrants from Russia, Ukraine, and other countries from the post-Soviet domain. This group includes some other traditional communities as well, such as the small in number but well-integrated Armenian community, which has attracted new immigrants looking for a more placid political and economic environment ambience than in their native countries;

• immigration from the Near and Middle East is an element in a nearly half-century old tradition: Syrians, Lebanese, Palestinians, Iraqis, Afghans, etc.;

- African immigration resembles the Arab group with respect of its continued presence in the country for almost half a century. However, its numerical strength is considerably lower, and it is symbolically perceived as different due to lack of historical contacts between Bulgaria and the African countries. Notably, immigrants from the Maghreb are very few in number and are incorporated into the Arab community;
- Chinese immigration is among the most recent migrant phenomena and started practically from scratch after the opening of the country in the early 1990s;
- the most recent but growing group comprises EU citizens who, according to European statutory norms incorporated into Bulgarian legislation, are not considered foreigners, and exercise their right of freedom of movement (Krasteva, 2011);
- to the enumerated migrant groups, migrant from older Bulgarian diasporas or Bulgarian natives can also be included. Of these, the most numerous is the group of the Macedonian nationals.

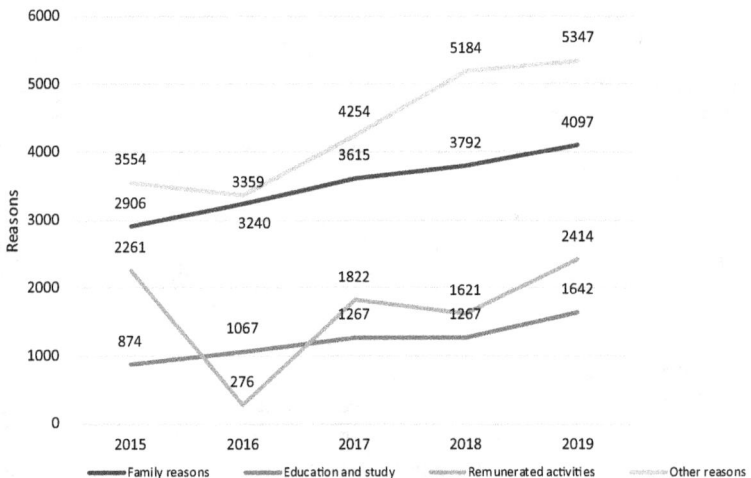

Figure 1.4 Residence permits granted during the year to third-country nationals by reasons and length of validity.

Source: Authors after data from the NIS.

For nearly a decade later, despite some changes in the dynamics and characteristics of the migration fluxes to Bulgaria, this typology has remained largely in force. It is evident that, although recent in character – mainly economic in nature – immigration into Bulgaria after 1989 is largely rooted in the pre-1989 years. What is interesting is the profile of the immigrants into the country and their level of integration. We will begin with labour market inclusion. Immigrants originating from the former USSR – among them already a second and a third generation – are occupied practically in all areas of the economic affairs, including state administration and such sectors as education. In the last years prior to the pandemic there was a tendency for seasonal employment mainly of Russian speakers in the branch of tourism. A new wave of Russians who have invested in property on the Black Sea coast which they use for holidays and rent out without settling permanently in Bulgaria. For the most part, immigrants in Bulgaria from Near and Middle East are self-employed or running small family businesses. The major areas of employment are petty commerce, restaurant business, or retail trade. These ethnic niches are occupied by Arabs, Afghans, Kurds but also Chinese. What is typical of many immigrants is that they are mostly employed by companies owned by other immigrants, and do not work for Bulgarian employers (Krasteva, 2013). A new form of employment are the call centres, attracting both members of Arabic-speaking communities and Western Europeans. As of 2013, Krasteva remarked that he level of unemployment (14%) is nearing the national average. One cannot emphasise enough that there is a greater number of unemployed migrants among the refugee groups than among immigrants. A pre-crisis survey revealed that 44% of all immigrants have full-time jobs, 11% work part-time, 6% are students, 4% are housewives, and 9% are retired (Georgiev, 2008). Most immigrants are occupied actively in the workforce; some of them are self-employed and many, in turn, have generated jobs for native Bulgarians. The professional status profile of immigrants is also very interesting: entrepreneurs represent 13%, managers account for 4%, "white collars" – 36%, free-lance professionals – 8%, workers – 31% (Georgiev, 2008; Krasteva, 2013).

The educational background of immigrants is also positive: 24% have a university degree and 59% have completed secondary education. Some of the migrants are highly educated because most of them have arrived during the 70–80s to study and later chose to settle in the country (Krasteva, 2013).

This positive picture has unfortunately changed over the years. This positive profile is attributable mostly to the fact that the genesis of a great portion of the migrant communities dates back to the pre-1989 years. It is not accounted for by specific policies, but by the small number of migrants who managed on their own to integrate into the society. Through the diversification of the migrant waves, especially after Bulgaria's accession to the EU and mostly after it found itself located on the Balkan Refugee Route, levels of inclusion did not improve but rather deteriorated. Nevertheless, one should consider that in view of the overall social and economic situation in the state, it neither attracts nor retains a high percentage of support-seeking migrants. This, however, does not exclude the necessity of devising such policies.

Speaking of migration, we should bear in mind that the availability of statistical data is crucial to the understanding of the relevance of different migration phenomena and migration policies. Looking at Bulgaria, there is no access to reliable and updated information (Krasteva, 2014). Although several local institutions provide data on different aspects of their migration situation, accessible and centralised system is accessible for collecting data on migration flows (Staykova, 2013; Krasteva, 2014). Mancheva and Troeva point out that the history of Bulgarian migrations of the post-1989 period is yet to be written. This can be accounted for by the process of gradual incorporation of relevant conceptual and methodological instruments of analysis on the part of social scientists and with the slow adjustment of the country's statistical systems to the needs of adequate examination of migration trends. Consequently, migration processes of the 1990s remained to a great extent unnoticeable to social scientists and Bulgarian institutions responsible for the governance of migration (Mancheva and Troeva, 2011).

Occasionally, our analysis also stumbled into problems stemming from missing data and insufficient accumulation of wider scope of academic research in the field. Nevertheless, it largely corresponds to the purposes of the present research.

Emigrants, who fear immigrants

Write Valentina Ganeva-Raycheva and Milla Maeva: "Determining the exact number of expatriate Bulgarians is a difficult if not an unachievable undertaking" (Ganeva-Raycheva, 2019, p. 342). A report released ten years after the accession of Bulgaria to the EU makes the following statement:

> For the entire period from 1985 to 2016 the population of Bulgaria has decreased by 1.85 million people. According to NSI[12] more than half (over 52%) is due to the negative natural growth

(the difference between birthrate and mortality rate), while 48% is due to net migration. Nearly half of the net migration is due to the expulsion of the Bulgarian Turks at the end of the communist regime.

(Angelov, 2017)

And again, in their estimate, between 1985 and 1992 the decline in population figures was entirely attributable to net migration, while in the next period the predominant factor was the negative natural growth rate. The share of net migration in the population decline has decreased to 39% in the period between 1992 and 2001, to 31% in the period between 2001 and 2011, and dropped below 10% for the period from 2011 until now (ibid). Ultimately, employing different data and methodology, the researchers have drawn the following conclusion:

According to official Bulgarian statistics, about 900,000 people left the country in the last three decades. According to data for other countries data the number of Bulgaria-born individuals who reside abroad amounts to about 1.1 million. The UN assessment [fixes] the number at 1.176 million but removing the difference for Turkey... results in [another] 1.1 million people. The differences can be explained by... differences in the timeframes, [varying] definitions for migration and inaccuracies. [It may be] accepted that the figure of those [who] left Bulgaria [amounts to] about 1.1 million people and that they [reside] mainly in the EU, Turkey, and the US. According to our estimate, between 600,000 and 700,000 people have left the country for economic reasons (ibid).

These data stand in drastic contrast to the evaluations uttered by politicians and the public attitudes on the subject. In the estimate of the Chairman of the Committee of Expatriate Bulgarians in the 44th National Assembly, Andon Dontchev, a member of the Will political formation,[13] there are two and a half million people residing outside the country (Welle, 24.10.2017), and the incumbent Chairman of the State Agency for Expatriate Bulgarians believes that for the period 2017–2018[14] they numbered over 6–7 million (actualno.com, 06.07.2016). The political discourse on the subject often projects emigration as a reason for demographic collapse and even as national catastrophe. This is the manner it is most often represented in the media as well. Titles such as *Half of Bulgaria Disappears by 2100* (24 chasa, 15.07.2020), *Migration, Death... We Dwindle by 50–60,000 Annually* (dnes.bg, 21.09.2020), etc., occur frequently whenever it comes about the demographic state of the country. Broad public circles join the media in imposing pessimistic interpretations and uttering doom for the future of Bulgaria and the Bulgarians. Thus, for example, scientists from the Bulgarian Academy of Sciences produced a report on commission from then Deputy Prime Minister Valeri Simeonov,[15] which reinforced the negative prognoses reflected in press headlines such as *BAS announces: The Extinction of Bulgarians Already Irreversible…* (24 chasa, 23.03.2018).

The recent years saw the unusual rise in popularity of campaigns to stimulate natality sponsored by certain circles close to the conservative and nationalist parties. Such is the "Do It Now" campaign of the National Cause Movement (the title's abbreviation reads as the Bulgarian for DNA),[16] which has provoked some more liberal circles to react describing its slogans as sexist and offensive, such as: "Your mother would fancy a grandchild more than a new kitchen pan", "Non-silicon C-cup", "Selfies with children garner more likes", and "Fatherhood can make you groovier". Organisers explained for the *Capital* newspaper that their aim was to attract attention from young people in reproductive age and to encourage them to start a family and have children in case they already happened to have met their partner, and if they felt unprepared to make an informed decision as to how long it is possible for them to postpone family planning, adding that the campaign was funded entirely through private sponsorship, with a large part of it secured by the organisers and the rest collected from successful Bulgarians who backed the initiative (Capital, 15.07.2019a). A next step in their commitment to handle the demographic situation in the country would be the Bulgaria Wants You campaign, which aims to support Bulgarian emigrants as they return to the country by extending assistance in their attempts to find realisation, because "We know that you love Bulgaria, and you miss it. Because you miss its air, its water, the scent of your favorite breakfast meal, the warmth of your native home…" Dr. Milen Vrabevski, a businessman and public figure is also committed to work along this line[17] via his foundation "Bulgarian Memory". In addition to initiatives in promoting natality, financing in-vitro procedures, families of many children and so forth, he is also engaged in support for the "Bulgarian diaspora in Ukraine, Moldova, Northern Macedonia, Albania and Serbia".

Although euphemistically qualified or concealed behind concepts like "responsible nativity" or "responsible parenting", these campaigns promote the birth of Bulgarian children and what is understood most often is ethnic ones. The position upheld by the IMRO[18] party is not so euphemistic, however, as they have repeatedly taken stance against the "gypsification" and the necessity of limiting birth rates for Bulgarian nationals of Romani origin. In its capacity of partner in the 2017–2021 government coalition, the party in the person of Krassimir Karakachanov, Deputy Prime Minister on security affairs and Defense Minister, submitted for endorsement a Conception for Changes in the Policy for Integration of the Gypsy (Romani) Ethnos in the Republic of Bulgaria and the Measures for their Realization (Council of Ministers, 2014), which makes the claim that "many gypsy woman use up almost entirely their working age period filling it with maternity leaves to bear and raise children. And in result, the number of people in this ethnos has increased considerably". The "Conception" goes on to suggest mechanisms to restrict what it calls "marginal natality devised to obtain social benefits".

It is in the same context that one can also view the mass campaign against the Istanbul Convention,[19] as well as the purported cases which received broad public resonance, of children of Bulgarian families alienated by the Social Services of Norway[20] and the campaigns rallied by parties and other public organisations against modifications in the Strategy for the Child[21] and the UN Global Compact for Migration,[22] which have become a commonplace reference for the menace against the traditional Bulgarian Family and the primordial values of society.

Thus, the talk centring on demographics and Bulgarians threatened by extinction, the enforcement of values alien to their tradition serves to spawn moral panics, steady clichés, and symbolic universes. In this respect Georgi Bardarov and Nadezhda Ilieva write:

> One of the serious problems regarding the demographic situation of Bulgaria, is the tendency to view it both in an arbitrary fashion and divorced from the demographic processes and changes in the developed world to which we belong. From this perspective, we focus on indicators and tendencies on which it would be difficult to have influence, and which certainly are not the main problem of Bulgaria. In our country there is a constant talk about the low birth-rate, the continuing record-low number of newly born babies for the time census statistics are kept and about population aging. All three are clichés diverting attention from real demographic problems.
>
> (Burdarov, 2018, p. 6)

Bardarov and Ilieva place these tendencies within a broader European context and draw the conclusion that

> the great problem of Bulgaria lays not in birth rate or population decline represented in absolute values, but in the emigration of

young people and hence – the demographic misbalance between younger and older inhabitants and an exceptionally high for an European country mortality rate, attributable to additional factors. On the whole, however, Bulgaria performs quite normally in the contemporary demographic tendencies of the developed world.

(ibid: 6–7)

It is also interesting to note that in their report they propose a range of recommendations for coping with the situation which presuppose not so much purely pro-natalistic policies, but rather the improvement of the overall public and political ambience in Bulgaria. Similar opinions can also be found during field work with Bulgarians living abroad, who have enumerated the stimuli for eventual return. Thus, for example, the recommendations of an Open Society report made as early as 2010 state that the importance of enforcing comprehensive reforms aiming at the improvement of education, healthcare, and security in Bulgaria should not be underestimated as a factor in the containment of emigration, since people do not emigrate solely for economic reasons (Ivanova, 2010).

The statement in the above paragraphs is not a gratuitous negation of tendencies which were also cited in the first section of this chapter.[23] Expanding into the demography debate has some relevance to the topic to the extent that it is an avenue to the understanding of the attitudes of Bulgarian society towards immigrants, mostly by enforcing the already mentioned "rendering" of migration in terms of condemnation, expectations of extinction, loss of identity, and superseding the traditional values by such as were imported from abroad. A similar conception is set forth in the book *The Light That Failed* by Stephen Holmes и Ivan Krastev:

we aim to show how the process of depopulation in Central and Eastern Europe that followed the fall of the Berlin Wall helped populist counter-elites capture their public's imagination by denouncing the universalism of human rights and open-border liberalism as expressions of the West's lofty indifference to their countries' national traditions and heritage.

(Krastev and Holmes, 2019, p. 26)

If Bulgarians have a traumatic experience with the perspective of their own extinction, the perspective of foreigners infiltrating into the society is experienced dramatically. The two are closely related. In this connection, Holmes and Krastev write: "Anxiety about immigration is fomented by a fear that unassimilable foreigners will enter the country, dilute national identity and weaken national cohesion. This fear, in turn, is fueled by a largely unspoken preoccupation with demographic collapse" (Krastev and Holmes, 2019, p. 64).

The tendency of discrepancy between the reality of data and the citizens' perception of the number of immigrants and their influence on the structure of society is valid for the most European countries. European public opinion significantly overestimates the number of non-EU immigrants: in 19 EU member states citizens perceive the proportion of immigrants as being at least twice the actual figure (European Commission, 2018). Particularly after the 2015/2016 peak in refugee arrival, the topic gained centre stage in the political debate with multiple consequences. Indisputably, misperceptions regarding the impact of international migration led to the polarisation of politics in EU Member States and to the rise of populist and racist political forces across Europe. At the EU level, this has given rise to the unprecedented and ongoing political crisis arising from the failure to find an agreement on the distribution of asylum seekers (Mudde and Rovira Kaltwasser, 2018). Hostility towards migration also negatively affects citizens' attitudes to social redistribution in general (Alesina et al., 2018). Reflecting significant variations between countries, attention centres on how to limit the impact of migration, rather than on devising a governance to tap the development potential of migration in the countries and regions of destination.

In Bulgaria this trend is mostly manifest in the country's eventual location upon the Balkan Refugee Road after 2013. According to a study by Alpha Research Agency, 83% of the Bulgarians have voiced some apprehensions that the rising number of refugees might involve risks to the country's security. The gravest concerns were occasioned by refugees rioting in protest of the living conditions in accommodation facilities – 39%, and by the fact that in comparison to the local population, asylum seekers and / or refugees were more tolerated by the state – 37%. A bare 17% of respondents fail to see a serious reason to worry (Alpha Research, October 2013). A sociological research by the same agency from September 2016 shows 61% of Bulgarians to find migrants the ultimate external threat to national security (Alpha Research, September 2016), and according to the Eurobarometer from November 2016, 77% are opposed to the resettlement of third-country nationals on Bulgaria (European Commission, Autumn 2016).

A 2018 investigation by the European Commission reveals Bulgarians to be the most intolerant to migrants of all EU member states

(European Commission, 2018). A mere 15% of the respondents then gave a positive answer to the question whether they would accept to have a migrant as a colleague, doctor, neighbour, or to enter their families. By this index, Bulgaria is at the top place in the EU. In comparison, the same research shows 57% of the people in the EU to be fully in favour of working with and making the acquaintance of migrants. Two-thirds of the population of Spain, Sweden, Ireland, Portugal, and the Netherlands has a positive attitude. The analysis of the data shows Eastern Europeans to be more sceptical. A curious element of the research is the level of awareness. It seems that apart from being the most intolerant, Bulgarians are the least informed – a bare 17% have some knowledge of the issue. The assumptions are that foreigners residing in Bulgaria number about 11% of the population, exceeding many times over the official statistics. The same research reveals that over 90% of Bulgarians do not have migrants as personal acquaintances, have not spoken with any of them or have not even seen any of them. Nevertheless, they believe that migrants could endanger them by taking away their jobs or by being a burden to the social welfare system. Half the respondents find that migration poses problems and 6% perceive it as creating opportunities. The perception of Bulgarians radically differs from opinion prevailing in the EU, where over 70% believe migration could provide a boost to economy. Overall, Bulgarians are sceptical about immigrants being in position to enrich them culturally by contributing to local music, arts, cuisine, and crafts (European Commission, 2018).

Interesting data on the social distancing from foreigners are cited by a joint research of UNHCR and BAS (UNHCR and BAS, 2020), which focusses on refugees and people seeking international asylum. It corroborates some of the observations outlined in earlier researches, but they give rather distinctive prominence to the fact that the lack of first-hand information leads to attitudes based on entrenched stereotypes and information shared on the media. In this sense it should be noted that media play a central role in shaping the public opinion on foreign nationals in Bulgaria and at the same time they have the responsibility to provide reliable information on the subject in accordance with the professional principles of journalism.

In the next chapters we shall gradually complete this puzzle to construct an overall analysis of how the overlapping media interpretations, political discourses, and narratives concerning migration in the context of dominant populism make impossible the making of policies and place Bulgarian society in a situation of permanent post-truth reality.

Notes

1 Kiryakov quoted a report of the Minister of internal affairs to Politburo, stating that by the end of the 1970s, 10,500 citizens of the People's Republic had illegally left the country (Kiryakov, 2011).

2 In the early 1980s certain circles within the Central Committee of the Bulgarian Communist Party enforced the conception of the necessity of changing the names of "Bulgarian Turks". The first stage of the campaign was carried out in the winter of 1984–1985 under strict secrecy. Nearly 1 million citizens were forcibly compelled to change their Turkish names to Bulgarian (Eminov, 1997). Every instance of resistance was overcome through violent methods (Eminov, 1997). After 1985, the purpose of the communist regime is the full and total integration of the Turkish minority into Bulgarian culture. A restriction was enforced against using Turkish language in public places. On 18 May 1989, actions of protest started against the policy of the government. In consequence to mounting public pressure, rulers found themselves compelled to make an extreme decision for the solution of the "Turkish problem". As a result, many intellectuals, underground Turkish leaders active at the time, or future ones, were forced to leave the country. As a next stage, over the Bulgarian Television there was announcement that "Bulgarians who have been converted to Islam and want to visit Turkey, would receive passports if they request to have one" (Eminov, 1997).

3 It is likely that the number of those leaving might have been greater, if Turkey had not closed its border (Eminov, 1997). It should also be stated that immediately after November 1989 and in the following years around 150,000 people who had emigrated to Turkey during the "Grand Excursion" returned to Bulgaria.

4 Amendments in the Foreign Travel Passports Act, made earlier in relation to the "Grand Excursion" state: "Every citizen of the People's Republic of Bulgaria shall have the right to leave the country and to return to it with a Bulgarian foreign-travel passport or a substitute document" (Promulgated in State Gazette, No. 38, 19 May 1989; effective as of 1 September 1989).

5 Thus, for example, there is an interesting transformation in the migration of Bulgarian nationals from Turkish origin, which from forced and ethnic was transformed into labour migration and diversified its destinations but will not be specifically examined in this text.

6 It should be considered that experts note the real size of migrant transfers to be considerably greater. It is believed that no less than 30% of remittances are being effected outside official channels, and in countries in immediate proximity to the country where the emigrants are employed, this share may exceed 50%.

7 BNB data show that there was a drastic decrease for all the months of 2020 after January and February.

8 Deneva explains the genesis of these processes with policies of the regime prior to 1989 (Deneva, 2014).

9 The protests began on 14 June 2013 as a reaction to the election of Delyan Peevski from the Movement for Rights and Freedoms as a Director of the State Agency for National Security. MRF has come to be steadily perceived by the public opinion as a symbol of backdoor politics and

corruption, with Delyan Peevski who – apart from being a member of the party – has serious business interests, for example, in the media but in numerous other sectors as well, has become the face of the mafiotised state. The protests were spontaneously organised on the social networks, mainly Facebook. They gained prominence under the hashtag #DANSwithme (In Bulgarian, DANS is the abbreviation standing for the State Agency for National Security and when pronounced in Bulgarian is homophonous with the English word "dance"). The protests lasted for nearly 400 days in varying numerical strength. Significant role in them was played by Bulgarian nationals from abroad, with protest actions almost continually organised at many places outside Bulgaria. Many who had returned to the country for the summer months were actively involved in the processes.

10 The 2020 protests began on July 9 with demands of the resignations of Prime Minister Boyko Borissov and the Attorney General, Ivan Geshev following a series of events, which had started with suspicions raised by the procedure followed in the election of Geshev and claims that he had been "appointed" by Peevski himself. Protests then proceeded with an action of the leader of one of the extra-parliamentary opposition parties against illegal construction development and "seizure" of Black-sea beach for private housing project of the MRF Ahmed Dogan and ended in an incursion of officials of the Prosecutor's Office into the presidential institution following charges brought against members of the cabinet of the head of state, with charges dropped by the court of the first instance. They received support from opposition-backed President Rumen Radev, who on several instances took part in them and invented the motto "Out with the thugs!". Many young Bulgarians, who had made a return to the country due to restrictions relating to the Covid-19 pandemic, also became involved in the protests. Campaigns were also organised outside the country.

11 Thus, for example, this analysis does not treat the exceptionally important issue of the generation of children who have remained in Bulgaria, while their parents are working abroad, or those who, on account of transient or circular migration, have dropped from the educational system or attend school sporadically.

12 National Statistical Institute

13 "Volya" ('Will') is a political party which exists under this title since 2016 and was formerly known also as "Dnes" ('Today') and "Liberal Alliance". The leader, the businessman from Varna, Vesselin Mareshki, is famous for his assets mainly in pharmacy (owner of a chain of drugstores) and the fuel trade (owner of fuel stations). The party was a member of the populist coalition "Order – Legality – Equity" in 2012. On the 2017 parliamentary elections he appeared individually, passing the 4% threshold and acceding to the National Assembly. Unofficially, but through several actions he lent support to the GERB-UP coalition (2017–2021).

14 Petar Haralampiev is the president of the BG Patriot Alliance, which lent support to the United Patriots Coalition, officially founded for the 2016 president elections, which at the time of its inception included the National Front for Salvation of Bulgaria (NFSB), IMRO, Ataka, Middle European Class, and the Union of the Patriotic Forces "Zashtita" ('Defense'). He is closely associated with the IMRO and was nominated for Chairman of the State Agency for Expatriate Bulgarians in 2017 when the UP became the

junior partner in the third GERB government (2017–2021). In 2018, Petar Haralampiev was incriminated as a leader of a criminal group linked to the illicit purchase of Bulgarian passports, mostly to Macedonian nationals. Later gained notoriety in the public domain with photographs of himself sporting a T-shirt with inscription reading "Wehrmacht".

15 Valeri Simeonov is a businessman and politician. His career started in the 1990s in the Union of Democratic Forces, and later he went in to found the Ataka Party together with Volen Siderov. Owner of the SKAT Television, which played a crucial role in the advance of the party. Following the local elections he was elected chairman of the Municipal Council in Burgas in coalition with the GERB Party. In January 2009 he submitted his resignation on account of the decision voted by the majority of municipal councillors to endorse the erection of a mosque in a neighbourhood of the city. After a series of public scandals with Siderov he left Ataka to found the NFSB. Initially of regional importance in Burgas, the party later joined the coalitions Patriotic Front – NFSB / IMRO (2014) and the United Patriots – IMRO / NFSB / Ataka (2017). In his capacity of a member of Parliament and from the Parliamentary tribune, he described the Roma people as "raging anthropoids", and their wives as "having the instincts of streetwalking bitches". On 4 May 2017 he was elected Deputy Prime Minister of the economic and demographic policy in Boyce Brasov's third government (GERB – United Patriots). In October 2018 he called the mothers of the children with malfunctions "clamorous females with allegedly sick children". This sparked another wave of protests, which continued for over a month and he was compelled to submit his resignation. Simeonov returned to the National Assembly and shortly afterwards was elected its vice-chairman. On the parliamentary elections of 2021, NFSB appeared in coalition with Vesselin Mareshki's "Volya/ Will".

16 He is backed by TV producers known as Ivan and Andrey (Ivan Hristov and Andrey Arnaudov) who make no secret of their "patriotic" disposition and fondness for parties from the nationalist description. In addition to all that, they also produce television programmes devoted to the preservation of traditional Bulgarian values and morality. They also have an active position of Macedonia and the "protection of the Bulgarian interests there".

17 His business interests are localised mainly in scientific research and developmental activity in clinical medicine. In addition, he runs a private school and finances the erection of monuments of medieval Bulgarian rulers, such as Samuil, disputed by Bulgaria and Macedonia, whose monument was erected in the centre of Sofia. He is considered a close figure to GERB and parties from the nationalist register.

18 IMRO-BNM (Interior Macedonian Revolutionary Organization – Bulgarian National Movement), a self-identified successor of the historical Interior Macedonian Organization, formerly Internal Revolutionary Organization for Macedonia and Odrin (founded in 1893 with the purpose of liberating the Bulgarians who had remained within the boundaries of the Ottoman Empire in the aftermath of the Treaty of Berlin from 1878 which governed the establishment of the Principality of Bulgaria). It resumed activity in the 1990s and since 1997 is active as a political party.

Over the years the party has participated in various ad hoc coalitions with varying success. It had members of parliament after the parliamentary elections in 1997, 2005, 2014, and 2017. The leader of the party, Krassimir Karakachanov, remained on ninth position on the 2011 presidential election, but ended third in 2016. In 2014, on the election for the European Parliament, the IMRO appeared in coalition and had one representative in the EU (and another one for the coalition partner). In 2019 appeared individually and won two seats. As a part to the Patriotic Front coalition – NFSB / IMRO, it lent support to the third Borissov government. In the 2017 United Patriots coalition – IMRO / NFSB / Ataka, it became junior partner in the government and had ministers in the cabinet (2017–2021).

19 In July 2018, the Constitutional Court declared anti-constitutional the Council of Europe Convention on preventing and combating violence against women and domestic violence, better known as the Istanbul Convention. The decision was preceded by social hysteria, enacted from the outset by IMRO representatives, but afterwards broadly discoursed by representatives of all political parties that the aim of the Convention was to impose the "gender ideology" (it should be considered that Bulgarian uses the same word for 'sex' and 'gender'), same-sex marriages, and values untraditional to Bulgarian society. The topic continues to be relevant even to-date, finding its way eve in the electoral campaign for the 2021 parliamentary election.

20 Norway and its social services Bernvernet found their way into the public debate in Bulgaria following a series of media reports presenting biased accounts of estranged children of Bulgarians living there. It did note take long before mass psychosis was aroused, with a range of Facebook groups emerging for the defence of Bulgarian children, and politicians joining the discourse. In certain predominantly Roma quarters under the influence of evangelical churches (see next footnote), but not only, parents went so far as to take their children right from the school class or to withdraw them altogether from attending school for fear that "Norwegians are coming to take them away". The case of the "Norwegians" is an emblematic example of a false news and living in post-truth situation.

21 After the "Norwegians", the topic of the endangered Bulgarian children continues to be relevant, with the Strategy for the Child being the new target. Politicians from IMRO and other parties, non-governmental organisations, and circles associated with the evangelical churches have joined forces in attacking a document, aiming at the improvement of the country's child protection system. Particularly active was certain evangelical pastor, who holds a second job as a public-relations officer at the Ministry of defense, with minister and deputy prime minister the leader of IMRO.

22 The Migration Pact is another document, after the Istanbul Convention, which fell under the blows from Bulgarian nationalists. Especially active is the IMRO representative in the European Parliament, Angel Djambazki.

23 A very on-topic and extensive research of demographic trends featuring texts dedicated to emigration and Bulgarians abroad in their demographic dimensions is titled *Measures for Overcoming the Demographic Crisis in the Republic of Bulgaria. Volume III Migrations and National Identity* (BAS, 2019). Our analysis does not lay claim to exhaustiveness in this respect, its rather aims at positioning the emigration narratives within the overall context of politicisation of migration and populism.

Bibliography

24 chasa, 2018. *24 chasa.* [Online] Available at: https://www.24chasa.bg/ novini/article/6786607 [Accessed May 2021].

24 chasa, 2020. *24 chasa.* [Online] Available at: https://www.24chasa.bg/ novini/article/8812510 [Accessed May 2021].

actualno.com, 2016. *actualno.com.* [Online] Available at: https://www.actualno. com/society/6-7-mln-bylgari-jivejat-v-chujbina-news_620919.html

Alesina, A., Miano, A. and Stantcheva, S., 2018. *Immigration and Redistribution.* s.l.: NBER.

Alpha Research, October 2013. *Societal Attitudes.* s.l.: Alpha Research.

Alpha Research, September 2016. *Societal Attitudes.* s.l.: Alpha Research.

Angelov, G. and Lessenski, M., 2017a. *10 Years in EU. Migration Trends in Bulgaria.* Sofia: OSI-Sofia.

Apostolova, R., 2017. Duty and debt under the ethos of internationalism: The case of the Vietnamese workers in Bulgaria. *Journal of Vietnamese Studies,* 12(1), pp. 101–125.

Atanasova, E., 2005. Rusnatsi [Russans]. In: A. Krasteva, and A. Krasteva, ed. *Imigratsiata v Bulgaria [Immigration in Bulgaria].* Sofia: IMIR, pp. 156–191.

BAS, 2019. *Measures for Overcoming the Demographic Crisis in the Republic of Bulgaria. Volume III Migrations and National Identity.* Sofia: Marin Drinov Publishing House of BAS

Bobeva, D., 2004. *Capital.* [Online] Available at: https://www.capital.bg/ politika_i_ikonomika/bulgaria/2004/12/11/229189_parite_na_emigrantite_ sa_stimul_za_ikonomicheskiia/ [Accessed 10 May 2021].

Bulgarian Citizenship.com., n.d. *Restoration of Bulgarian Citizenship.* [Online] Available at: http://www.bulgarian-citizenship.com/restoration- bulgarian-citizenship/ [Accessed 20 March 2021].

Burdarov, G. I., 2018. *Horizont 2030. Demografski tendentsii v Bulgaria.* Sofia: Friedrich Ebert Stuftung.

Capital, 2019a. *Capital.* [Online] Available at: https://www.capital.bg/biznes/ media_i_reklama/2019/07/15/3938503_vijte_tazi_kampaniia_i_napravete_ dete/ [Accessed May 2021].

Capital, 2019b, August 8. *Capital.* [Online] Available at: https://www.capital. bg/politika_i_ikonomika/bulgaria/2019/08/09/3949227_kolko_bulgari_ jiveiat_v_evropa/ [Accessed 21 January 2021].

Capital, 2019c, August 9. *Koloko bulgari jiveiat v Evropa.* [Online] Available at: https://www.capital.bg/politika_i_ikonomika/bulgaria/2019/08/09/3949227_ kolko_bulgari_jiveiat_v_evropa/ [Accessed 10 May 2021].

CLS, n.d. *Litsata na romskata migratsia po sveta.* Sofia. [Online] Available at: http://www.cls-sofia.org/bg/projects/state-of-society-18/-119.html.

Council of Ministers, 2014. *Council of Ministers. Portal for Public Consultations.* [Online] Available at: https://www.strategy.bg/PublicConsultations/View. aspx?lang=bg-BG&Id=4289 [Accessed 14 February 2021].

Deneva, N., 2014. *Conflicting Meanings and Practices of Work. Bulgarian Roma as Citizens and Migrants.* Sofia: Collective for Social Interventions.

34 (Re)discovering migration

Deutsche Welle, 2017. [Online] Available at: https://www.dw.com/bg/колко-българи-са-емигрира- ли-в-чужбина/a-41083550 [Accessed May 2021].

Ditchev, I. (2003). Usiadane na nomadskia komunizum. Sotsialisticheskata urbanizatsia i krugovete na grajdanstvoto. [The settlement of nomadic communism]. *Sotsiologicheski problemi [Socilogical problems]*, (3–4). dnes.bg., 2020. *dnes.bg.* [Online] Available at: (https://www.dnes.bg/obshtestvo/2020/09/21/migraciia-smyrt-topim-se-s-okolo-50-60-000-dushi-godishno.463542) [Accessed May 2021].

Eminov, E., 1997. *Turkish and Other Muslim Minorities of Bulgaria*. London: HURST&COMPANT.

European Commission, 2016 Autumn. *Standard Eurobarometer 86*. s.l.: European Commission.

European Commission, 2018a. *Eurobarometer Survey 469: Integration of Immigrants in the European Union*. s.l.: European Union.

European Commission, 2018b. *Together against Trafficking in Human Beings, Bulgaria.* [Online] Available at: https://ec.europa.eu/anti-trafficking/member-states/bulgaria_en [Accessed 14 February 2021].

European Commission, 2021, February 15. *Bulgaria: Twice as Many Receive Bulgarian Citizenship Compared to 2019*. [Online] Available at: https://ec.europa.eu/migrant-integration/news/bulgaria-twice-as-many-receive-bulgarian-citizenship-compared-to-2019 [Accessed 20 March 2021].

Eurostat, 2020. *People on the Move. Statistics on Mobility in Europe. 2020 Edition*. [Online] Available at: https://ec.europa.eu/eurostat/cache/digpub/eumove/index.html?lang=en

Eurostat, 2021, January. *Migrant Integration Statistics – Housing*. [Online] Available at: https://ec.europa.eu/eurostat/statistics-explained/index.php/Migrant_integration_statistics_-_housing#Home_ownership [Accessed 20 March 2021].

Ganeva-Raycheva, V. M., 2019. Bulgarskite obshtonosti zad granitsa i tehniat demografski potentsial. In: K. Vladimirova, ed. *Migratsii i natsionalna identichnost*. Sofia: Marin Drinov, pp. 337–383.

Georgiev, O., 2020. *The Grand Return: COVID-19 and Reverse Migration to Bulgaria*. Sofia: ECFR Sofia, in cooperation with Konrad Adenauer Stiftung.

Georgiev, Y., 2008. Immigration to Bulgaria – Preconditions and possible developments. In: Y. Georgiev, ed. *The Implication of EU Membership on Immigration Trends and Immigrant Integration Policies for the Bulgarian Labor Market*. s.l.: EIP.

Hristova-Balkanska, I., 2012. Socialno ikonomichesko razvitie na ES 27 i na Bulgaria. In: *Bulgarskata emigratsia: teorii, politiki, empirichni izsledvania*. Sofia: Ikonpis, pp. 93–127.

Investitor, 2017. *Investitor.bg*. [Online] Available at: https://www.investor.bg/ikonomika-i-politika/332/a/zapochva-proces-na-obratna-migraciia-na-bylgarite-248748/ [Accessed 2 February 2021].

Ivanova, I., 2010. *Tendenzii i transgranichnata migracia na rabotna sila i svobodno dvizenie na hora – efecti za Bulgaria*. Sofia: Open Society Institute.

Ivanova, Y., Stoilova, Z., and Santova, A., 2019, September 10. *How Many Bulgarians Live in Europe?* [Online] Available at: https://www.europeandata journalism.eu/eng/News/Data-news/How-many-Bulgarians-live-in-Europe-And-what-are-the-trends-in-their-mobility [Accessed 13 February 2021].

Kalchev, Y., 2012. Demografski, socialen i ikonomicheski profil na bulgarskite emigranti. In: BAN, ed. *Bulgarskata emigratsia: teorii, politiki, empirichni izsledvania.* Sofia: Ikopis, pp. 147–172.

Kamenova, D., 2005. Africantsi [Africanse]. In: A. Krasteva, ed. *Imigratsiata v Bulgaria [Immigration in Bulgaria].* Sofia: IMIR, pp. 74–88.

Kiryakov, B., 2011. *BKP i politikata kum emigratsiata.* [Online] Available at: http://ebox.nbu.bg/anti/ne3/7%20B._Kiryakov._Balgaria_zad_granica_NBU%20+.pdf

Kokinu, M., 2012. Bejantsite v Bulgaria ot grajdanskata voina v Gurtsia: izsledvane na ketegoriata "bejanets" [Refugees in Bulgaria after the civil war in Greece]. *Sotsiologicheski problemi [Sociological problems],* 1–2, pp. 275–293.

Krastev, I. and Holmes, S., 2019. *The Light That Failed. Why the West Is Losing the Fight for Democracy.* s.l.: Penguin Books.

Krasteva, A., 2005. *Imigratista v Bulgaria [Immigration to Bulgaria].* Sofia: IMIR.

Krasteva, A., 2013a. *Bulgarian Migration Profile.* [Online] Available at: https://annakrasteva.wordpress.com/2013/03/21/bulgarian-migration-profile/ [Accessed 8 March 2021].

Krasteva, A., 2013b. Digitalniat grajdanin – politicheskiat prokekt na internet revolutsiata. In: A. Krasteva, ed. *Digitalniat grajdanin.* Sofia: Nov Bulgarski Universitet, pp. 7–16.

Krasteva, A., 2014a. Bulgarian migration profile. In: F. Medved, ed. *Proliferation of Migration Transition. Selected New EU Member States.* European Liberal Forum, pp. 189–211.

Krasteva, A., 2014b. *Ot migratsia kum mobilnost. Politiki i putishta.* Sofia, Bulgaria: Nov Bulgarski Universitet.

Krasteva, A., 2016. *Balkanskiat migratsionen fenomen.* [Online] Available at: https://annakrasteva.wordpress.com/2016/0 [Accessed 9 May 2021].

Krasteva, A., 2019. *The Bulgarian Migration Paradox.* Sofia: Caritas Bulgaria.

Krasteva, A. S., 2011. *Satisfying Labor Demand through Migration in Bulgaria 2004–2009.* Sofia: European Migration Network.

Maeva, M., 2006. *Bulgarskite turtsi – preselnitsi v republika Bulgaria [Bulgarian Turks].* Sofia: IMIR.

Mancheva, M. and Troeva, E., 2011. Migrations to and from Bulgaria: The State of Research. In: M. Hajdinjak, ed. *Migrations, Gender and Intercultural Relations.* s.l.: IMIR, pp. 17–68.

Mineva, M., 2018. *The Faces of Roma Migration to the EU.* s.l.: Centre for Liberal Strategies.

Mitseva, E., 2005. Vietnamtsi [Vietnamise]. In: A. Krasteva and A. Krasteva, ed. *Imigratsiata v Bulgaria [Immigration in Bulgaria].* Sofia: IMIR, pp. 89–105.

Mudde, C., and Rovira Kaltwasser, C., 2018. Studying populism in comparative perspective: Reflections on the contemporary and future research agenda. *Comparative Political Studies*, 51(13), pp. 1667–1693.

OECD, 2019. *International Migration Outlook 2019*. Paris: OECD.

Office to Monitor and Combat Trafficking in Persons, 2021. *2020 Trafficking in Persons Report: Bulgaria*. [Online] Available at: https://www.state.gov/ reports/2020-trafficking-in-persons-report/bulgaria/ [Accessed 14 February 2021].

Petkova, D., 2014. *Pochti polovinata migranti sa zaplasheni ot bednost*. [Online] Available at: https://www.investor.bg/evropa/334/a/pochti-polovinata-imigranti-ot-treti-strani-v-es-sa-zaplasheni-ot-bednost-184282/ [Accessed 20 March 2021].

Petrunov, G., 2014. Human trafficking in Eastern Europe: The case of Bulgaria. *The ANNALS of the American Academy of Political and Social Science*, 653(1), pp. 162–182.

Research Center Trend, 2020. *Attitudes of Bulgarians towards Emigration (Нагласи на българите спрямо емиграцията)*. Sofia: Research Center Trend.

Staykova, E., 2013. Emigration and immigration: Bulgarian dilemmas. *SEER: Journal for Labor and Social Affairs in Eastern Europe*, 16(4), pp. 403–415.

Sultanova, R., 2006. Bulgarite kato bejantsi [Bulgarianse as refugees]. In: A. Krasteva, ed. *Figurite na bejanetsa [The figures of the refugee]*. Sofia: NBU, pp. 151–177.

UNHCR and BAS, 2020. *Survey on Public Attitudes towards Refugees and Asylum Seekers in Bulgaria 2019–2020*. s.l.: UNHCR.

2 Post-1989 migration policy in Bulgaria on paper and in practice

This chapter is focussed on policies relevant to migration after 1989 through several chronological and analytical entries: in the first place, there was a prolonged absence of any kind of policy and construal of migration as an issue of political order in the early years of democracy. In the second place, in the fast development of several strategies and plans as a result from Bulgaria's accession to the EU which, however, failed to generate sustainable migration policies and laid the foundations for an ethnocentric, primordial, and securitarian understanding of the phenomenon. In the third place, in the years after 2012/2013, which not only reinforced the securitarian "rendition", but sharply introduced migration into the political debate in the context of predominant populist discourse. Methodology proposes document analysis and political programmes alike, as well as analysis of the media. The hypothesis is that narratives about migration originate precisely through the discourse of politicians, media, and other public actors and that these narratives, mixed into the existing public attitudes, mutually intensify each other generating an overall environment of post truth, permanent sense of crisis and impossibility of developing policies and actual management of the processes, which should guarantee sustainability and social cohesion for Bulgarian nationals and migrants alike.

Non-policy which is not a policy and strategy production

Not just the migration panorama, but also the treatment of the phenomenon in Bulgaria is radically different from those before the 1989. If the totalitarian regime aimed to eliminate or at least to limit maximally both emigration and immigration, post-Communist Bulgaria naturally prioritises freedom of movement for citizens and the observance of their rights and freedoms. There is an attempt to establish

DOI: 10.4324/9781003161493-3

certain balance between these principles and the regulation of migratory flows, mostly as far as irregular migration is concerned, and this has become more conspicuous in the context of the EU accession process. Eugenia Markova defines several strategic policy goals:

> improvement in the management of economic migration; increasing border security in view of taking on regional responsibilities for the protection of the external borders of the EU; protecting the rights and promoting the integration of legal immigrants in Bulgaria; international cooperation and compliance with international treaties on migration (Ministry of Labor and Social Policy, 2004). In an attempt to stem undocumented migration since 1991, several bilateral agreements for employment of seasonal or temporary workers were signed.
>
> (Markova, 2010)

Most researchers, however, agree in the understanding that in the first years following the democratic changes the State failed to recognise migration as a matter of political order (Krasteva, 2014). Abiding by the understanding that "policy making begins with the identification of a public problem that calls for a policy response (see e.g. Bacchi, 2008)" (Breugel, 2020), then what is lacking in the case of Bulgaria is the identification of a public problem involving political response, whereas other goals are being pursued. Research on national migration policy models at European level not infrequently refer to the "non-policy" or about the "laissez-faire" model. In the case of Bulgaria, it would be difficult to refer to these models (Geddes and Scholten, 2016), insofar the lack of policy is not a consequence of recognising a cluster of public issues or of a conscious political choice, that is, what is missing is not just policy, but conceiving migration in political order. And if some political objectives have been eventually identified, they are found in the periphery of other public policies or as a result of other, more dimensional foreign-political projects.

What proved a factor in the crystallisation of migration to the status of public policy was Bulgaria' accession to the European Union. In this sense, Vankova and Draganov write:

> Before Bulgaria's EU accession process commenced, asylum and migration policies were largely neglected. By 2007, the country had fully harmonized its legislation on migration in line with the EU acquis (Nedeva, 2017, p. 25) and had laid the foundations for the development of Bulgarian migration policy. A national

public policy in the field of migration was established, however, only after the accession of Bulgaria to the EU (Krasteva et al., 2011, p. 11).

(Vankova and Draganov, 2020)

The development past this moment is particularly interesting: after the accession, the State has produced several strategic documents on migration. The national Strategy for Migration and Integration (2008 – 2015) is the first document which brings it nearer to the definition of migration policy with two major goals:

• attracting people of Bulgarian citizenship residing on the territory of other countries, and of people of Bulgarian origin but with foreign citizenship, for permanent return to the Republic of Bulgaria.
• achieving and implementing adequate policy on reception and integration of foreign nationals and enforcing of efficient control over migration flows (2008).

It is evident that the promoted vision regarding migration is highly ethnocentric – the return of the new Bulgarian emigration and attracting of foreign citizens from Bulgarian origin. Only after these purely ethnic reasons follow the economic considerations: the second target group is defined as "third-country citizens with qualification answering the needs of the sectors of Bulgarian economy, which experience shortage of workforce" (2008). The main emphasis is placed on the immigrant as a purveyor of direct foreign investments. In a 2011 analysis, Krasteva draws a general conclusion:

Bulgarian approach unfolds in the primordial perspective. It stems from the premise of strong identities by origin and individual migration projects whose aim is to manifest these identities – for the Diaspora representatives who want to settle in Bulgaria in order to return to their land of origin and contribute to its development. However, [as we can see] from theory, and as proved in practice, the main motivation for migration is pragmatic; and identities are being instrumentalized to achieve not cultural but economic goals.

(Krasteva et al., 2011)

"Economic" logical models, however, can also be encountered on another level – producing policies with the purpose of utilisation of European funds and resources. Vankova writes:

The first, the National Strategy on Migration and Integration (2008–2015), claimed to set the grounds for the development of a consistent national policy on managing migration and integration. In fact, one of the main reasons for creating a strategy in this field could be found in the establishment of the EU general program on "Solidarity and Management of Migration Flows" and the available funds for all EU Member States.

(Vankova and Draganov, 2020, p. 117)

In 2011, just three years after the first, the country adopted another National Strategy in the Area of Migration, Asylum and Integration (2011 – 2020). It defines three main goals:

- prevention and effective counteraction to illegal migration.
- more effective governance of economic migration and integration.
- redefining migration and mobility into positive factors of development in economic and demographic aspect (2011).

As revealed by the two strategies, Bulgaria is intent to pursue a selective migration policy, with the desirable types of immigrants explicitly defined. If in the initial Strategy primordialist logics coexist with economic reasoning, the second offers amalgamation between ethnicity and security. The enforcement of a new, securitarian, type of logic could be explained with the specifics of the period when the document was produced – it coincides with the definition of the country's membership in the Schengen area as a major priority in the country's foreign policy and the beginning of preparations for this process. Thus, the ethnocentric, yet inclusive approach of the initial document, coached in verbalisations such as attracting, reception, and integration, is replaced by the notion of governance understood in terms of prevention and counteraction (Krasteva, 2014).

Implementation and accomplishment of the objectives projected into the strategies, is envisaged to be accounted by means of annual reports and further activities are to be outlined again in the annual action plans. Surprisingly, according to the portal for public discussion of the Council of Ministers where these documents are published[1] there is an account from 2011, an action plan from 2013, which however is not accounted for, and no action plan is developed for the next year 2014. Thus, it turns out that after the accelerated development of a new strategy in 2011, migration was quickly jettisoned from the priorities of the government in Bulgaria and although a document was in existence defining it as a public policy, it has remained only in paper while it is missing as a practice.

A new document appeared in 2015, which covered the period of the one from 2011. The National Strategy in the Area of Migration, Asylum and Integration 2015–2020 aims at:

> ... creating a political framework for the establishment of a complex and sustainable statutory and institutional foundation for efficient governance of legal migration and integration, as well as for prevention and counteraction of illegal migration and for identification and granting the necessary care for seekers and recipients of asylum in Bulgaria.
>
> (2015, p. 5)

The document also stresses that "...the policy of the Republic of Bulgaria in the area of migration, integration and asylum is based on the national interests and the coordinated approach of the EU member states and the fundamentals of international law" (2015, p. 6). The strategy derives no less than 12 points of priority. Even this high number suggests the main purpose of the document – to cover as many aspects of migration policy as possible and mostly – to be in complete unison with European documents, standards, and values. The new situation, stemming from the war in Syria and the opening of the Balkan Refugee Route, did not trace a route to the top positions in the hierarchy of priorities in Bulgaria. These were occupied steadily by such priorities as are relevant to the country's inclusion in the Schengen Zone membership. Seeking to "appeal" to European partners and institutions is distinctly perceivable by the fact that "combating corruption"[2] has found its way even into a document defining migration policies. In the beginning of 2021, without debate or media coverage, a new strategy was adopted. It was prepared with a post-crisis perspective and in view of migration pressure from previous years, the debate of the new European migration policy, asylum and health situation. It is not a coincidence that Bulgaria's new National Strategy on Migration for 2021–2025 drops the term "integration" from its title. It distinctly emphasises as priority the tendency of maximum control over migration. In its best part the text deals issues related to border control, repatriation of nonregulated migrants, work with the countries of origin. The part related to integration is formulated as "conditions of migrant admission" (p. 5), without specifying what kind of conditions are meant (p. 20). With respect to the integration of immigrants already residing in the country no measures are designated, but there is a reference to the practically not working programme for integration of people who have received asylum. What makes impression is that this strategy also designates the qualified migrants as a target group for attracting to the country. Even more interesting is the approach employed in attaining this goal which is reduced to benign regime of entry and residence in the context of mobility. The last strategy of the county in the area of migration pays very little attention to specific Bulgarian migration panorama. It focusses much more in the European dynamic in the area which is associated with a revision in the general policy, intensifying of the selective approach and work with specific problems. Thus, for example, the Bulgarian strategy places a focus on then work with unaccompanied foreign minors. This confirms the articulated tendencies.

The institutionalisation of the migration phenomenon was equally chaotic as the manufacturing of strategies. In Bulgaria, different institutions and ministries oversee various aspects of migration within their own sphere of competence. In addition, the National Council on Migration and Integration was established in February 2015 as a collective coordinating authority for the formulation, adoption, and implementation of State policies and action plans on migration and integration. It is co-chaired by the Minister of Interior and the Minister of Labor and Social Affairs. The rest of its membership comprises representatives of other State authorities. In 2019 this council was superseded by new National Council on Migration, Borders, Asylum and Integration.

The main reason for this institutional reform is the requirement laid down in the European legislation for establishment of a national mechanism for integrated border governance.

In conclusion, Bulgaria's migration policy has some peculiarities, which can be periodised as follows:

- period of ignorance and neglecting (1989 – 2007) – migration issue is almost not articulated; the immigrant integration is left entirely to immigrants to handle on their own. A different element of migration governance can be found in certain laws, but on the overall it reflects a conservative approach. A possible explanation of this situation may have to do with the relatively small number of foreigners, the foreigners' background, as well as the emigration profile of the country.
- period of recognition and rapid development of documents (2008 – 2015) – mainly within the context of EU accession, migration was introduced on the political agenda and discourse. From almost non-existent migration governance, governments

rapidly developed several national strategies reflecting the inconsistency in the approach to management – ranging from the highly positive appreciation of migration as a development resource to a more securitarian approach. Positive steps associated with integration policies during this period relate mainly to the procedure of synchronisation of legislation with the EU acquis. The downside to it is that these steps have remained on paper only.

• period of halt in migration governance (2015 – until the present day) – paradoxically, following the outset of the so-called European migration crises, integration governance in Bulgaria almost came to a halt. Governments continued to draft and elaborate documents, but implementation procedures are missing. The Bulgarian Helsinki Committee voiced an even more extreme evaluation in a 2019 report, describing the year 2019 "a zero year in integration" (Bulgarian Helsinki Committee, 2019). This becomes most visible when the integration of refugees is being analysed.[3] One of the factors explaining the inactivity is paradoxically the high degree of politicisation.

Traditionally, we have accepted that migration policy comprises flow management policies and inclusion policies. The former affects the actual crossing of territorial borders, the latter – the transcendence of the imagined boundaries of the nation, after the famous definition of Benedict Anderson. Geddes provides a reminder that international migration becomes visible precisely through the borders of States – which are not just territorial but also organisational and conceptual boundaries (Geddes and Scholten, 2016, p. 4):

> whether international migration is viewed as a "good" or "bad" thing is heavily dependent on decisions made in destination countries and, as Zolberg (1989, p. 406) (Zolberg, 1989) evocatively put it, the walls that these countries build and the small doors that they open in these walls.

> (ibid)

Strategic documents in the area of migration clearly reveal that Bulgaria has built too many walls and opened very few doors. Conceptual walls – the perception of migration in terms of ethnicity compatible with Bulgarian nationality and along the lines of securitarian logic, ultimately produce few inclusion policies, as seen in the following lines, and the tangible representation of a wire fence, as we shall see in the next section of this chapter.

In the previous chapter we have outlined the profile of immigrants in Bulgaria as well-integrated, and primarily, as being included at the labour market. An interesting evaluation is featured in one of the major and most prestigious international researches regarding integration policies:

> Bulgaria's approach to integration is classified by the last MIPEX 2020 issue as "equality on paper". A lot of documents were produced, some of them with a very good quality, [but they have] remained without any practical "on ground" consequents. Major obstacles [have arisen] in nearly all areas of life, with few exceptions – of the labour market, permanent residence and anti-discrimination.
>
> (MIPEX, 2020)

The picture presented by some other researchers, however, is more critical. For example, the access of immigrants to labour market is assessed as restrictive and unsupportive. This policy has a limiting effect on the adjustment mechanisms of the economy and the labour market in favourable and unfavourable times. Labour market situation has worsened considerably due to negative demographic growth and the economy has suffered massive shortages of workforce, which tend to impede economic growth. There is an exception from the conservative migration policy trend – a recently introduced procedure of recruitment of short-term workforce for the tourism sector. Foreign workers are permitted to work up to 90 days within a calendar year and the employer is not obliged to submit documents of qualification of the candidate for work (Bobeva et al., 2019, p. 73). Differing interpretations are attributable to the fact that the research of Bobeva et al. was written from the perspective of the needs of the labour market proper, which is affected by workforce shortages.

Despite the general and mostly positive picture, it should be noticed that the situation with the foreign nationals in the country is mixed and complicated. Although the general conclusion is that for their most part migrants in the country integrate well, in the first place this is not the result of policies and in the second place, there are some significant differences between various migrant groups. Refugees, victims of human trafficking, minors and women tend to be much more vulnerable than the rest. One can infer that the situation became even more complicated after the Covid-19 pandemic.

Furthermore, the lack of clear vision addressing the specific needs of vulnerable migrants in the country greatly reduces the chances of resolving the issue. Another indicator, which is often closely related to other indicators of social exclusion and deprivation – more specifically, income-related – is the overcrowded rate. This is the reason why, when the relatively high level of poverty risk and the income inequalities in Bulgaria are taken into account, the EUROSTAT 2019 data for the overcrowding rate in immigrant households indicate that more than half the foreign nationals in Bulgaria (59.3%; low reliability) reside in overcrowded households (European Commission, 2021). A step forward is the 2018 amendment of the Labour Migration and Labour Mobility Act. It provides that family members of foreign nationals who have become Bulgarian citizens are entitled to the same social rights as any Bulgarian citizen. There are also noticeable positive improvements in the sphere of access to education. The Immigrants and their children no longer face impediments to their access to compulsory education and receive language support at school (MIPEX, 2020). However, the school system creates barriers to access for certain categories of immigrant pupils and largely ignores the specific needs and benefits they bring to the classroom (MIPEX, 2020). It should also be said that policies in the area of housing are totally missing.

Citizenship is another key institution in the governance of the migration and Integration policy of any State. The analysis of citizenship investiture policies should consider Bulgaria's specific experience with migration. In the case of Bulgaria, granting citizenship is understood more as a result than stipulation for successful integration of migrants. The standard naturalisation procedure requires that any applicant spend at least ten years in Bulgaria before submitting application for citizenship. In addition, applicants are supposed to display financial independence and stability, as well as good command of the Bulgarian language. The commitment to Bulgaria is reinforced by the requirement to foreign nationals under general naturalisation to renounce former citizenship. As it will be made clear, this vision in the citizenship investiture governance is reflected on many levels – in legislation, on practice, in the discourse. According to statistics, there have been for the past few years the same top five countries of origin for those who acquired Bulgarian citizenship: the Republic of Northern Macedonia, Ukraine, Serbia, Moldova and Albania (European Commission, 2021). Turkish nationals have shown some interest in obtaining Bulgarian citizenship which has remained stable for years. There is a trend for citizenship restoration of Turkish nationals who were divested of Bulgarian citizenship in the migration processes of the 1980s (Bulgarian Citizenship, n.d.). There is also a substantial increase, resulting from the so-called European migrant crisis, in the number of Iraqi and Syrian citizens who have received Bulgarian passports. Other instances of increase of third-country nationals pending investiture of citizenship in Bulgaria, are Vietnam and Armenia (European Commission, 2021).

In the context of Bulgaria's citizenship-granting policies it is worth mentioning the possibility for obtaining Bulgarian citizenship on the merit of investments made in the country. This possibility has already been available in Bulgarian legislation for decades, but its political instrumentalisation has acquired new dimensions in the last several years, during the tenure of the GERB-United Patriots government. Concerning existing possibilities, in 2020 Bulgaria received a letter from the European Commission which voiced misgivings regarding the regime for conceding citizenship in exchange for investments. Although similar regulations for "golden passports" are in place in many European states,[4] EC voices reservations for the procedures in only three States: Bulgaria, Malta, and Cyprus.

A closer focus on the policy of granting Bulgarian citizenship shows that it may possibly have other inherent drawbacks. Thus, for example, there is another procedure calling for attention – granting of citizenships for special merit. For the past ten years citizenship was obtained by 142 foreign nationals, mostly athletes.

Curiously, this procedure – like the procedure with the investment regime that we have already commented upon – is not public. Until now, with one exception dating from 2021,[5] the questions of who exactly is supposed to obtain Bulgarian citizenship for particular merit, were deflected with the argument that it is a matter of personal information. There is an ongoing debate in society and media about whether each case of granting Bulgarian citizenship should not be given publicity. After all, merit is a fine thing and it would be good if authorities went public with what they considered special service, whether it was about service to society or merit to somebody's private interest.

Another "shortcut" to obtaining Bulgarian citizenship has drawn some notice – not just public and in the media, but political as well. This is one of the issues, on which IMRO, one of the parties of the government coalition in power until 2021, have a clearly stated position related to attracting Macedonians of Bulgarian origin. In October 2018, Peter Haralampiev, Director of the Agency, and employees of the institution were detained during an enquiry investigating the illicit sale of fake certificates of origin. Haralampiev and three other people were accused of being members of an organised criminal group dealing in document frauds and bribery.

Because of the scandal in the State Agency for the Bulgarians Abroad (SABA), at the end of 2018 Prime Minister Boyko Borissov ordered an inspection of over 40,000 individuals who had obtained Bulgarian passports. This is the first instance of origin-based citizenship reception being commented in terms of possible malfeasance.[6] A Free Europe investigation of early 2020 found that despite disclosures following an inspection ordered by Prime Minister Boyko Borissov dealing the issuing of Bulgarian passports to foreign nationals without meeting conditions of the procedure, the issued passports were not recalled, as required by law.

An attempt to improve the performance of the outlined Bulgarian citizenship-granting system was reflected in the decision, voted in connection with the adoption of the Law for Amending and Supplementing the Law of Bulgarian Citizenship from 2021, which we have already commented upon, to rescind the requirement in the naturalisation procedure which stipulates that the application for obtaining of citizenship be accompanied by a certificate of Bulgarian origin, issued by the State Agency of Expatriate Bulgarians.

According to the new statutory arrangement, documents used by the individual to certify that he / she has an ascending relation up to and including third degree of Bulgarian origin, should be submitted directly at the Ministry of Justice along with the application for acquisition of Bulgarian citizenship.

Apart from the apprehensions of defalcation with the citizenship-granting policy, its being politically controlled and corrupted, the problems described undermine the integrity of the status of EU citizenship. Such schemes have implications for the EU and upon citizenship being granted by the State, the recipient becomes an EU citizen and benefits from all rights, for instance of freedom of movement, residence and work in the EU, the right to vote on elections for local municipal authorities and for the European Parliament. The consequences are neither restricted to the states implementing these decisions, neither are neutral as far as other states are concerned.

In purely theoretical terms, the character of the citizenship-granting policies fits well into the conception of "immigration choisie". In practice, however, it is more about corruption practices and not about real political conceptualisation of migration.

Government approach concerning migration is of consequence because its policies can influence whether integration would work as a two-way process in the country. The way governments treat immigrants has a very strong influence on how well immigrants and the public interact with and what they think of each other. Bulgaria's current policies encourage the public to see immigrants as equals but also as aliens (MIPEX, 2020). In deep analysis, the case of Bulgaria shows that the problems stem not so much from deficiencies in legislation or from specific policies – such as the policy for providing access to education or business opportunities – but from the political context of populist securitisation which undermines the potential of immigration and integration policies and shapes a negative public opinion (Krasteva, 2019, p. 31).

Models of integration are rather a theoretical and useful division, which can be viewed in the sense of Weber's ideal types, but actual State policy seldom belongs to just one type. Very often, the assimilation model operates in only one section of migration policy, whereas the multicultural, to name one example, is engaged in another. However, it is not the only reason why it is difficult to answer to which integration model the policies implemented in Bulgaria can be assigned. It is easier to identify the model they would not be assignable to.

Possibly on account of the relatively low percentage of migrants in the country, and due to their profile, the State has failed to invest in the development of integration policies in the initial years following the democratic change – policies similar to those which for a long time have prevailed in traditionally immigration countries, like, for example, the development of special educational programmes for immigrants; inclusion of an immigrant representative body in local and national bodies of authority; permitting double and multiple citizenship; financing the migrant organisations as a way to support of cultural activities; financing the bilingual education in the maternal tongue, etc. As we already had the opportunity to say, migration has not been recognised as an issue from the political order, which explains why in reality there is no actual debate as to what integration model should be applied as regards migrants.[7] On the other hand, the country has contributed global experience by generating experience of its own once migration is assigned a policy status. The political vision of integration is synthesised into the so-called "integration by origin". This formulation, which has no corresponding theoretical analogue but has a distinctive primordialist ring, can be found in the first Strategy from 2008. It explicitly formulates as a matter of national interest the active attraction mostly of foreign citizens of Bulgarian origin, since they are regarded as individuals integrated by origin (Council of Ministers of the Republic of Bulgaria, 2008). Subsequent documents stick with this logic. It is to remain unclear, though, how is the country supposed to handle the individuals of non-Bulgarian origin. Among a huge number of different ministries and establishments involved in one way or another in the process of migration governance there is not a single government institution with the specific purpose to accomplish the social integration of immigrants into the country. After the country found itself located on the Balkan Refugee Route, (un)expectedly fewer policies began to be implemented in this area.[8] It is hardly an accident that a mission of the European Economic and Social Council, after a visit to the country and meetings with representatives of institutions and the non-government sector, concludes in its report: "In Bulgaria, a proper strategic framework guiding integration actions does not exist" (European Economic and Social Council, 2019).

More and more politics, fewer and fewer policies

Anna Krasteva wrote in 2013:

> Politicization of migration is still to come to Bulgaria. In opposition to numerous EU countries with strong anti-immigration parties and crucial role of discourses on immigration in political campaigns, new migration countries like Bulgaria do not face these challenges. There are no extremist or right-wing parties exploiting migration themes. The extremist party with the symptomatic name "Attack" mobilizes anti-minority rhetoric against Roma and Turks, not against migrants.
>
> (Krasteva, 2013)

Defining immigration is political matter (Geddes and Scholten, 2016). Krasteva has summarised two approaches to migration policy – the one has politicians "take the temperature" of public opinion and on this basis formulate priorities and measures to be taken; the other, labelled "evidence-based", seeks support in the medium of science (Krasteva, 2014, p. 484). As stated on another occasion, migration research in Bulgaria is not well developed and policies in this area emerge only at a later stage. It is hardly surprising, given the context, that scientific research does not underlie policymaking. Politicians, however, tend not so much to "take readings" as to "give raisings" to the temperature of public attitudes, and just a few years after 2013 when Krasteva wrote the quotation used in the opening of this chapter, we have reasons to assert that the subject is highly politicised.

The refugee crisis evoked a completely new situation in which perceiving migration as a threat has become a steady symbolic universe. Apparently, the tendency for radicalisation of citizens was quickly instrumentalised by political actors. These two trends, however, act like interconnected vessels and mutually reinforce each other. Populist and extremist parties are most successful in exploiting the topic in resonance with societal attitudes, but they are not alone in enacting this type of mindset. Neither have any of the traditional political parties offered a viable alternative, rather on the contrary – they have reinforced the closed-border policy and intensified the anti-immigrant discourse. The topic dominated two electoral campaigns, although Bulgaria serves as a transit country, with anti-migration rhetoric ranging between ethno-nationalism to welfare nationalism.

In 2008, upon the adoption of the first migration strategy, Bulgaria had a coalition government comprised of the Bulgarian Socialist Party[9] and the centrist liberal parties[10] NDSS[11] and MRF.[12] Subsequently, or from the onset of the new situation, stemming from the country's location on the Balkan Refugee Route, even until early 2021, seven governments have been in power consecutively, which largely suggests a discontinuity in policies. Paradoxically, although such discontinuity is indeed in evidence, there is no fundamental difference in the conception as to what these policies should look like. The 2011 Strategy, which started the enactment of the securitarian logic, was developed by the GERB government, is dated before the outbreak of the new contingency with the increased numbers of asylum seekers. The 2015 Strategy was created in the outset of the new situation and in the context of an incipient politicisation process. This prevalent perception of migration in terms of security, restriction, control, closure has its own visible physical representation. The construction of the fence along the border with Turkey began in October 2013 and ended in 2017. In the intervening years, it became a source of continuous political scandal, where debates, rather than focussing on the essential issue of the actual need for the fence to be installed, were preoccupied with issues such as its construction cost, conformity to quality standards, or suspicions of corruption and inadequate efficiency:

> In October 2017, the Deputy Prime Minister publicly acknowledged that migrants continued to enter through the border fence with Turkey using ladders and that corruption among the staff of the Bulgarian border authorities has contributed to the increase of human trafficking.
>
> (Otova, 2017, pp. 16–17)

The statement is in line with reports from asylum seekers who claim that that Bulgarian Border Police officers have repeatedly facilitated migrants trespassing the EU's external border in return for a bribe (idem). A documentary released in November 2017 by a member of an opposition party showed that migration control along the Bulgarian-Turkish border was being enforced selectively, while also challenging the efficacy of the border fence as well as providing facts about refugee trafficking in the direction of Europe via Bulgaria, allegedly with the co-operation of the Border Police (idem).

Migrants and even some official institutional representatives have reported in numerous conversations[13] of traffickers hanging around accommodation centres and all this happening with the full awareness of the authorities (idem). In this respect, the politics of closed borders have a one-way effect – into the interior of the country; the going out of the country of asylum seekers is tolerated, even encouraged. In this respect, the politics of closed borders, within which the securitisation concerns have surfaced, paradoxically find a physical visualisation in the wire-netting installation, the subject of extensive political talk but yet to be installed in practice,[14] while ingresses into the country are still possible due to corruption while migrants leaving the country are tolerated by the authorities and even encouraged.

If an unconscious consensus that migration does not constitute a political issue seemed to prevail in the first years after 1989, in the years after 2015–2016 political actors took turns in debating on the subject. The "refugee crisis" quickly became a major internal political issue in Bulgaria:

> Although the number of people applying for or having received refugee or humanitarian status on the territory of Bulgaria is relatively small, their presence excited the spirits and gave rise to a populist surge in the media and among the political forces. (...) Refugees and asylum seekers given a start to a competition between the political parties in Bulgaria, who were competing to take a firmer stand than the others and proposing more restrictive policies regarding migrants with the intention to cash on the misgivings rampant in society. At least by this indicator Bulgaria has already come to resemble many of the "older" EU member states, where similar dynamics is not a yesterday thing. The threat of the foreigners is being exploited not only by extreme nationalist formations and the far right, but also from the mainstream parties, including those with declared leftist-centrist positions.
>
> (Bechev, 2017)

To trace this process of politicisation of the subject, we will use an extensive material from a media monitoring covering several electoral campaigns (2016, 17 and 19), positions voiced online and documents from sessions of the National Assembly, the Council of Ministers, and other institutions. European studies understand politicisation as the process of attributing significance to an issue of public interest via diverse channels such as media and political discourse, as well as a multiplicity and variety of the opinions pertaining to it being in evidence (Wilde, 2011, 2016). Our hypothesis is that the process of politicising of the migration topic in Bulgaria is taking place not in the context of a broad public debate involving a variety of viewpoints, but on the contrary – by propagating negative speech and within dominant populist discourse. Political actors have extensively exploited the topic, themselves often becoming the source of fake news and generating a sense of ongoing crisis in the process even after crisis levels have been surmounted.

We have opted for a chronological presentation of the events, following in parallel the political process and other processes occurring inside societal attitudes because these tendencies mutually reinforce and fuel one another, generating the overall situation wherein populism coexists with post-truth.

On 12 November 2013, President Rossen Plevneliev and Prime Minister Plamen Oresharski came issued a joint statement amid a series of incidents and assaults on migrants in the country (Council of Ministers of the Republic of Bulgaria, 2018). The symbolism of this act was exceptional, as just a few months earlier President Plevneliev had withheld confidence from government of Oresharski amid some of the most massively attended civil anti-government protests in the democratic history of the country.[15] This statesmanship, however, failed to set the tone of subsequent events.

For months to follow, what became the effervescent topic in the periphery of the societal and political debate was precisely the dynamic of the political process. It is present in the campaigns for the parliamentary elections and the elections for European Parliament but failed to be the leading motif of these campaigns. Tensions mounted in society were intensified. Thus, for example, on 26 April 2014, 17 Syrian nationals, holders of humanitarian status, among them six children were driven away from Rozovo – a village in the vicinity of Kazanlak, Bulgaria. The refugees arrived a few days earlier to the village where they had rented a local house. Their presence in the village sparked protests from local inhabitants. The protests took place in front of the lodgings and were accompanied by hate speech and threats of physical assaults. A report of one of the leading television stations, Nova, shows local villagers hanging a Bulgarian flag on the fence of the house where the migrants were accommodated, and shouting: "Bulgaria to the Bulgarians!" (Hristova et al., 2014).

(Not)surprisingly, the autumnal parliamentary session in 2015 was opened with two declarations delivered in the plenary hall. The one, from 4 September, originated from the BSP, and the second, from 11 September, from the Patriotic Front. Being already in opposition at the time, BSP vehemently berated the government party with demands for increased control on the borders, the EU for the lack of coordinated approach and set the trend which was to unfold and become increasingly distinctive in the coming months, of talking about migration as a burden on social systems. Disguised in phrases like "human drama" and ostensibly humanitarian arguments such as those related to human trafficking, it was at this stage already that the new and (a)typical for a leftist party conservative tendency had crystallised. The Patriotic Front, in the provocative tone typical of far-right populist formations, highlighted migration as a threat: hundreds of thousands of young men invading the European continent. The menace was economic, demographic, and especially cultural, because immigrants carry other traditions, mores, values; they are people unwilling to integrate into local communities, which have offered them their hospitality. Neither EU nor European politics is spared of criticism, with paradoxical arguments of concern for other communities: the absurd and unwarranted notion that mandatory relocation quotas would distinctly discriminate the citizens of North Africa and the Middle East seeking asylum and welfare. Due to the significantly differing economic standards of EU member states, immigrants will be put at a distinct disadvantage if compelled to settle in Turnu Măgurele or Batanovtsi, rather than in Paris or Berlin (see (Krasteva, 2018).

Meanwhile, the topic steadily established itself on the media, which played an essential role in generating the surging moral panic, which had also engaged besides politicians other public figures as well. One can cite a lot of examples, but we will focus on a debate between two of the most prominent political commentators, associated to the right and the left wing – Ognian Minchev and Andrey Raichev. Speaking on a programme at one of the most watched television stations, deliberating on the quota allocation, Ognian Minchev extensively explained that it is harmful to the Bulgarian national interest with Raichev concluding that: "Refugees see the situation at this continent in terms of naked women and free meal. They have come to your place and not just make a mess, but squabble and fight" (offnews, 24.09.2015) (see Dodov, 2015). Media also play essential role in stepping up the salience of the topic and if politicisation from above happens via politicians, analysers, and other actors with accepted authority, the one coming from below is being realised via a character which is novel to the Bulgarian society – the vigilante. Broad media prominence was given to actions of detaining foreigners performed by several, as later was made clear, criminally active "businessmen" with dubious occupations. Incidentally, some media were vociferous in calling them "superheroes", while broadcasting smartphone-filmed footage of actions of detaining, showing people lying on the ground with hands tied (BBC, 30.03.2016). It was against this background that the country entered the electoral campaign for president. In the period of the Presidential election campaign (September – December 2016), there were more than ten protest rallies against the accommodation of migrants held at various places, among them refugee locations such as Sofia Ovcha Kupel and Harmanli,[16] joined by other municipalities, such as Varna, Burgas, Russe, Samokov, and Yambol, which did not have any facilities of the kind. In some cases, the coordination of such protest rallies used the straightforward support of representatives of political forces (those from the Patriotic Front; later called United Patriots) or from formal and informal nationalist movements (the National Resistance Group,[17] or groups associated with the so-called 'refugee hunters'); other cases involved representatives of certain mainstream political parties including the BSP. The leader of one of the member parties in the United Patriotic Front commented on this occasion: "We were not fomenting, we organized the citizens' protest" (Vesti, 28.11.2016). Voices from within these parties also maintain a definite stance as to where accommodation facilities for migrants should be located:

> We insist that [refugee] camps be located on the border strip guarded by the military, outside populated settlements and [that they should be] of the closed type. How sensible would it be to encamp illegal migrants, overtly aggressive and unmanageable [folk], within mere meters of schools, universities, and kindergartens, as is the case with the Ovcha Kupel [facility] in Sofia?
>
> (*Flagman*, 18 September 2016)

Fears accumulated in society facilitate populist and nationalistic parties, making them recognisable to some as defenders of the national cause. At the same time, the same parties deftly fuel and amplify civil fears, generating an extra sense of insecurity and incapability, often resorting to the fabrication of fake news or exaggerating the existing risks. 'Waves', 'huge masses' which will effectively 'replace the genetic pool' – all this phrasing pertains to the verbal weaponry used to intensify these perceptions. The candidates in the campaign staked very seriously on the migration card. We will quote a sample of the discourse of the main candidates. The candidate pair of the United Patriots,[18] Krasimir Karakachanov, deployed a broad range of arguments against the migrants: not a single cent from the taxpayers' pockets should go to immigrants. Bulgaria is not a participant to this conflict (dnes.bg, 1.11.2016); There is an enormous danger of migrants flooding Bulgaria. A great part of them belong to terrorist organisations. Our border must be guarded both through a fence and by a service force (24chasa, 26.11.2016). The BSP-backed candidate, Rumen Radev, general and former military pilot, commander of the Bulgarian Airforce, became the star in the campaign. He had risen to political stardom some weeks earlier and was also quick to seize the moment and to instrumentalise the migration topic. Here is a sample of his position on topic: we should insist on the revocation of the Dublin Agreement because otherwise Europe will send back to our country the migrants registered here; it is necessary to announce a quota for the number of people who can be granted refugee status by our country (offnews, 26.09.2016); we should know if there is a scenario for permanent settlement of refugees, or to use European funds to finance additionally refugee camps and where our demography can be determined by the import of foreigners; there must be guarantees changes to Bulgaria's ethnic composition, values, demography, and religion are not forthcoming (cross, 29.09.2016); as it turns out, the 160-million allotment from Europe is projected to contain serious allocations for the sustenance of migrants; rulers intend to replace our expatriate children with refugees (bulpress.info, 30.10.2016).

There is a barely discernible difference in the discourse of the far-right and the left-wing candidate. It is evident from these statements that both politicians advance ethno-primordialism, welfare nationalism, and securitarian logic. A special emphasis is placed on the "replacement of the genetic bank" and the substitution of migrants for emigrated Bulgarian children.[19] The candidate of the incumbent government party, Tsetska Tsacheva, having formerly occupied the position of Chairwoman of the National Assembly, in contrast to the vehement anti-European discourse employed by her opponents adhered to a different rhetoric expected to sell better with Bulgaria's EU partners: to deal with the refugee crisis, it is necessary to have effective common foreign and security policy – something which is consistently upheld by Bulgarian institutions including the Parliament (inform.bg, 15.09.2016); the institutions are in their places, acting in coordination with each other. We utilise European solidarity – this is something very important. The strong voice of Bulgaria and its government is heard among the European institutions, and this works in the interest of the citizens (24chasa, 20.10.2016).

It is interesting to note that Krassimir Karakachanov was also a presidential candidate in 2011. He managed to garner just 33,236 votes, or 0.99%. In 2016, support for him increased to 573,016 votes, or 14, 9%. Despite of his ending third and failing to appear on runoff, this was a remarkable leap in the support for a far-right candidacy.[20] General Radev won the election and the GERB government submitted its resignation, which starts off another electoral campaign. Of course, it would be a speculation to assert that the results were attributable only to the deployment of the migrant topic, but its role should not be underestimated. At the same time, "focusing solely on parties and electoral politics risks underestimating certain phenomena, while exaggerating others. For example, a focus on electoral results may lead to the exaggeration or misinterpretation of the power of far-right parties" (Mondon, 2020, p. 213). What is of essential importance is the difficulty in distinguishing the discourse of the candidates of the far-right from the mainstream candidates, as the approximation does not go from the former to the latter, but vice versa.

The relevance of migration was sustained into the 2017 Parliamentary Electoral Campaign. Meanwhile the protests against migrants continue. One case that achieved significance in the spring of 2017 was the reaction of townsfolk in Belene towards an asylum-seeking Syrian family resettled in the town and towards a local Catholic priest who had lent support to them. This was not a singular incident of this kind. Some weeks earlier, similar incidents had occurred in some minor townships such as Elin Pelin and Shiroka Lyka.

We had an occasion to mention the role of European integration in the policymaking process. Now we may examine in more detail the tendencies in the political discourse.

In periods of intensive discussions on quota allocation, Bulgarian society fell repeatedly into confusion over conflicting statements made in Brussels by government officials compared to political discourse intended for domestic consumption. The so-called "hotspots" are an emblematic example. On 24 September 2015, the Prime Minister availed himself in an unprecedented way of his right of television-aired address to reassure the nation that no deployment of hotspots across the country was forthcoming and that he had defended the national interest at the session of the Council of the European Union held one day earlier. Chancellor Angela Merkel, eventually, broke the leading news from the forum: Bulgaria had advanced of its own accord the proposition to allow the instalment of hotspots across its territory. The opposition was likewise inconsistent in its usage of language custom-tailored to the varying junctures of foreign and domestic discourse: we call this "Brussels talk vs. Belene talk". In this respect, the leader of the Socialist Party often invokes migration in rather critical terms:

> Until now, it was Merkel who was telling [migrants] to come [to her country] and receive help, but now it is Borisov inviting them to come and avail themselves of dwellings, schools, a personal physician, social insurance and employment. This is a direct invitation for [migrants] to start arriving, [a pledge] that we would have their living arranged for them...
>
> (cross.bg, 27.09.2016)

Meanwhile, Sergei Stanishev, President of the Party of European Socialists since November 2011, MEP since 2014 and chairman of the Bulgarian Socialist Party from 2001 to 2014, upholds a very different position:

> We need to develop a coordinated action plan with the EU to cope with the increasing influx of migrants. (...) Although tending to beget challenges, migration can still offer numerous opportunities for the enrichment of our continent in its cultural, economic, and social aspect. Migrants can play a vital role in reviving the economy of aging Europe.
>
> (offnews, 10.10.2013)

Within the Bulgarian Presidency of the Council of the European Union (1 January–30 June 2018), member states have failed to reach a decision on the revision of the Common European Asylum System (CEAS) and this happened in 2020 during the German Presidency, with the process being far from conclusion.

An account of the presidency tenure, however, was given in the Bulgarian National Assembly, (not)surprisingly attended by a debate devoted precisely to migration. The issue was the subject of detailed discussions on two parliamentary sessions, one of them the meeting for parliamentary control. The verbatim statements cited below were enunciated by figures from various political parties, both in power and in opposition (National Assembly, 2018a).

Boyko Borisov, Prime Minister:

> Considering where our problem lies, I should tell you that the real problem is not with illegal, but with legal migration, since with

[the documents] we signed upon accession to the European Union, the Geneva Convention and all that, any individual who arrives at our border and shows up at an official checkpoint requesting asylum, we are obliged to grant asylum to that individual. From the moment this document is issued to the individual, this individual is considered "ours" – I say "ours" in the sense that in case he is denied reception in Germany or Austria or so on, there is nowhere else he can go [but to return to us].

Volen Siderov, Ataka Political Party (United Patriots):

As for the summit on migration, I believe there is no one here, in this hall, whether from opposition or governing parties, if they would be straight-thinking statesmen, to claim that [the summit] was not a success for Bulgaria, provided that we have explicitly declared that we have no wish to be a buffer zone. If we stick to this position in the future, and if it receives the support of each and every party in parliament, then it is bound to yield some results for Bulgaria. Moreover, if the head of state, elected in a direct vote by the people, also joins in this support, I believe that the effect will be even greater.

Cornelia Ninova, BSP [addressing the government in the capacity of leader of the opposition]:

You have nothing to say, because Bulgaria has no position [on the migrant problem] – no such thing was voted by parliament; no such thing was adopted by the Council of Ministers. What we have here is [the prime minister's] personal emotions and intentions, [articulated] in conformity with the dictates of the current juncture. [When he talks] here, in Bulgaria, he would have none of [the migrants] come, but with Merkel he is all for their coming. Therefore, we insist on more statesmanship [on his part], as well as to have a resolution voted by the Parliament of Bulgaria and of the Bulgarian Council of Ministers.

Upon a motion from the Socialist Party, the debates concluded with a vote on a three-point resolution:

The National Assembly (...) has RESOLVED:

1　The Council of Ministers is charged to refrain from signing any bilateral agreements concerning re-admission of migrants.

2   The Council of Ministers is tasked to submit to the National Assembly a position concerning the general (joint) resolution of the European Union on migration issues.

3   The Council of Ministers is charged to submit to the National Assembly Bulgaria's proposals for alterations to the so-called Dublin System for the reception of refugees and in particular Regulation (EU) No 604/2013 of the European Parliament and of the Council from 26 June 2013.

All 177 members of parliament in attendance of the session signed the resolution (National Assembly, 2018).

Apart from their ignorance of the topic, the internal coalition relations between GERB and the United Patriots and the exchange as a matter of course of accusations between ruling party and opposition, the debate has exposed also very clearly the lack of fundamental differences with respect to the migration policies, which crystallised in this (not) surprising ad-hoc majority.

Practically there was no electoral debate of the 2019 European Parliament elections campaign where migration was not a leading topic, while various topical issues were being articulated in the public domain for months prior to the campaign. In this respect, we cannot help agreeing with Mondon & Winter that:

> The media, both left and right, regularly runs stories about immigration being a main concern of the electorate. While outlets do not agree on how this issue should be tackled, they have mostly accepted that voters will identify immigration (and the construction of the other) as a key concern.
>
> (Mondon, 2020, p. 285)

April 2019, in the eve of the electoral campaign, began with information of the construction of new refugee accommodation centres. The *Sega* newspaper came up with the following title: "Amid Zero Migration Pressure the Ministry of Interior Roused Fears of Refugees" and announces, "zero migration pressure" and "no likelihood of accommodating refugees in the country". Amid resounding allegations, the ruling circles managed to rouse fears of a coming wave of refugees, sparking a new scandal just before the European elections. The inhabitants of three townships near the Bulgarian-Turkish border found out accidentally that the Interior Ministry is planning to build new centres for accommodation of illegal immigrants there. In Elhovo, where the largest of the camps was to be located, no one had ever heard about it.

Mayor Peter Kirov made a statement for the bTV that he learnt about the procedure from the website of the Public Procurement Agency. Protests were not long in coming. Residents of Malko Turnovo blocked the border crossing point for half an hour in demonstration of their reluctance to have a refugee camp around. The opposition even saw a conspiracy: "We want to ask the ruling party whether information is being withheld from the Bulgarian public about the return of migrants to Bulgaria from Western Europe, for the most part from Germany", stated the left-wing member of Parliament, Elena Yoncheva. The procedure for the construction of new camps was in a state of information blackout (The *Sega,* 1 April 2019).

Just three days later, at a regular Parliamentary Control session, Mladen Marinov, Minister of the Interior, announced that there was increasing migration pressure coming from Greece (The *Trud,* 6 April 2019).

The scenario continued to be relevant in the following days, too, with various actors involved in its articulation – the Military Minister and IMRO leader assured that should it be necessary, the Army would intervene in the situation (The *24 Hours,* 10 April 2019), and analysts from the "Trend" Research Centre were perplexed as to why the Co-ordinating Council for Internal Security was not summoned for a session to address the topic (The *24 Hours,* 10 April 2019).

Meanwhile, a criminal incident involving Bulgarian citizens of Roma origin, prompted Prime Minister Boyko Borissov to conclude: "We had migrants for the previous election and now that there aren't any migrants, we must find other ethnic issues…" (The *Trud,* 13 April 2019).

Whether there were or there weren't any migrants, and whether new "waves" were imminent proved an issue difficult for politicians to determine.

An open letter of 9 July 2018 from MEP Angel Djambazki and the Municipal Councilor from Sofia, Karlos Kontrera, both from IMRO – a member party of the incumbent ruling coalition, says the following: "As a result form the severe pressure on our border and the incursion of a substantial number of foreigners, the capital was flooded by thousands of alien new-comers" (offnews.bg, 09 June 2018). What is interesting, however, is that mere days earlier Krassimir Karakachanov, Deputy Prime Minister and Minister of Defense, as well as Chairman of the IMRO, commented during a session of the Council of Ministers:

> I have made an inquiry via the SAR and the capacity of the camps for emigrants (sic) is occupied at barely 11 percent. There were

no new entries unlike 2016 when the capacity was full up to 103% and I believe that the government should take a stand on that and at least order the competent authorities to investigate who is organizing such campaign[21] since this is punishable under the Penal Code. This is an act of stirring up commotion, an attempt to generate tension in society and this, in my opinion, cannot go unpunished.

(mediapool.bg, 27 July 2018)

Talking on the topic is limited to the exchange of such remarks in which the difference between facts and false news is blurred and through which the sense of permanent crisis is instilled. As reminded by Mondon&Winter: "A sense of crisis and urgency is essential for ideas to make their way into the mainstream, as they require a derogation from prevailing norms" (Mondon, 2020, p. 220).

In the period 2014–2019, the migration topic found a stable place in the political debate but failed to provoke an essential one. The topic was politicised in the context of dominant populist discourse and in the conditions of diluted borderlines between facts and false news. The divorcing of the public conversation about migration reality made it a generator of permanent sense of crisis in society. It is also interesting that the more migration is politicised, the less policies are made, as we have seen in the first section of the text. Having difficultly and languidly made its way to a public policy with the release of the first Strategy in 2008, in result of the European membership of the country, without a political conversation on the subject and without its being present in any way whatsoever on the political agenda, after 2014 it rose abruptly to prominence as a dominant topic. The periods of most distinct presence of migration in the political discourse, however, coincide with those of freezing the policymaking in the area of migration, integration in particular, or of their failure, while the conversation is still missing – because the political actors do not vie to propose alternative visions, but to ensure who among them would give migration a more negative representation. The following chapter focusses mainly on the refugee phenomenon, since it is Bulgaria's location on the Balkan Refugee Route that became the factor triggering these new realities and processes and represents the most explicit demonstration of the two prevalent trends in Bulgaria's migration policy – the erection of walls and the construction of a border fence with respect to governance of flows and the stoppage of integration policies as regards the incorporation of migrants into national communities.

Notes

1 http://www.strategy.bg/
2 Bulgarian governments are traditionally subjected to criticism for the high levels of corruption in the poorest member state of the EU.
3 We will focus more specifically on the refugee problem on the following chapter.
4 A total of 19 EU countries apply schemes for granting residence right in return of investment – Bulgaria, Croatia, Cyprus, the Czech Republic, Estonia, France, Greece, Ireland, Italy, Latvia, Malta, the Netherlands, Poland, Portugal, Slovakia, Spain.
5 The case in question is of Dr. Abdullah Zargar, a doctor of Iranian origin, who works in the small Bulgarian town of Isperih. Following rumours in the media that the doctor, who put the local hospital on its feet, had been waiting for more than six years an answer of a started naturalisation procedure, Dr. Zargar received Bulgarian citizenship for special merit, in the media spotlight and with two ministers in attendance.
6 In 2016, Katya Mateva, in the capacity of director of the Citizenship Council, denounced corruption practices and the fact that for years thousands of false documents of Bulgarian origin were issued to Macedonians and Albanians in return for a bribe. Between 500 and 1,000 euros per passport were paid to obtain a Bulgarian identity document, and according to her, there were days when up to 200 similar cases were being processed.
7 There is some incipient debate with regard to the traditional communities.
8 In the following chapter we shall see that there were integration measures for asylum seekers and refugees, but they abruptly ceased to be applied once a larger number of migrants had entered the country.
9 The Bulgarian Socialist Party is a direct successor to the Bulgarian Communist Party. It was renamed in 1999 following a referendum among its membership. Member of the Socialist International since October 2003 and of the Party of European Socialists since April 2004.
10 We use this definition inasmuch they are associated with the ALDE.
11 The Simeon II National Movement was founded in 2002 by Simeon de Saxe-Coburg-Gotha (King of Bulgaria from 1943 to 1946, although due to his age he ruled through the Council of Regents, Prime Minister of Bulgaria from 2001 to 2005). In the period 2001–2005, the movement governed in coalition with the MRF, with two BSP members in the government. In 2005–2009, the movement participated in the coalition government with BSP and MRF. It was later renamed to National Movement for Stability and Progress. In the 2009 elections, the NMSS remained outside parliament.
12 The Movement for Rights and Freedoms was established on January 4, 1990, and Ahmed Dogan was elected its chairman. To-date he is an honorary chairman after he resigned from active position, and on the party congress of the same year he was targeted by an assassination attempt. In terms of genesis and as electoral base, it is associated with Bulgarian citizens of Turkish origin or professing Islam. That is why nationalist parties often challenge its constitutionality, insofar the Bulgarian constitution prohibits ethnic parties. The MRF is often identified as the reason for the affiliation of business and the state.

13 Authors have conducted numerous field interviews with representatives of institutions and migrants.
14 The actual decrease in the number of migrant entries on the territory of Bulgaria can be traced to a much greater extent to the relevant agreement concluded between EU and Turkey.
15 See footnote in Chapter 1 about the protests in Bulgaria in 2014.
16 More on accommodation centres in Bulgaria in the next chapter.
17 National Resistance is more or less an informal nationalist organisation. It has been linked to a number of attacks on foreigners, members of religious, ethnic and sexual minorities, and people of leftist persuasions. It made numerous attempts to position itself as a political force, the most visible being in 2013, when together with representatives of "Blood and Honor" tried to register a political party. After the active reaction of representatives from civil society organisations, authorities do not give permission for the registration. Over the years, together with other nationalist organisations and with the active support of representatives of the political party IMRO participated in the organisation of the famous Lukovmarch – a procession in memory of General Hristo Lukov (served as Minister of War 1935–1938, 1942 and until his death chief leader of the Union of Bulgarian National Legions, far-right fascist organisation, emulating in its entirety the fascist symbolism). Lukovmarch started in 2003, and over the years it became more and more multitudinous, with neo-Nazis from all over Europe beginning to join it. Despite numerous reactions of non-governmental organisations, Jewish organisations from around the world, embassies, etc., the institutional and political reactions to the event in Bulgaria have traditionally been extremely sluggish and timid. Only in 2020 the event is officially banned, but in reality it continues to be held.
18 Their presidential candidate pair represented two parties: Krasimir Karakachanov from IMRO and Yavor Notev from Ataka.
19 In Chapter 1 we spoke of the traumatic experience of migration by Bulgarians.
20 In fact, this is not the first breakthrough of a national populist leader in a presidential election. In 2006, Volen Siderov, the leader of Ataka, won 597,175 votes and ran in the runoff.
21 What is referred to here is the spread of false information in the media about mysteriously landing planes with migrants returned from Western Europe.

Bibliography

Bacchi, C., 2008.*Women, policy and politics. The construction of policy problems*. Los Angeles: Sage Publications.

Bobeva, D., Zlatinov, D., and Marinov, E. 2019. Economic aspects of migration processes in Bulgaria. *Economic Studies (Ikonomicheski Izsledvania)*, 28(5), pp. 55–88.

Breugel, I. v., 2020. *Towards a typology of local migration diversity policies. Comparative Migration Studies* 8, 23.

Bulgarian Citizenship, n.d. *Restoration of Bulgarian Citizenship.* [Online] Available at: http://www.bulgarian-citizenship.com/restoration-bulgarian-citizenship/ [Accessed 7 March 2021].

Bulgarian Helsinki Committee, 2019. 2019 as the sixth "zero integration year". [Online] Available at: https://www.asylumineurope.org/reports/country/bulgaria/content- international-protection/2019-sixth-%E2%80%9Czero-integration-year%E2%80%9D [Accessed 11 December 2020].

Constitution of the Republic of Bulgaria. [Online] Available at: https://www.parliament.bg/en/const [Accessed 3 March 2021].

Council of Ministers of the Republic Bulgaria, 2011. *National Strategy in the Area of Migration, Asylum and Integration, 2011 – 2020.* [Online] Available at: https://www.strategy.bg/StrategicDocuments/View.aspx?lang=bg-BG&Id=670.

Council of Ministers of the Republic Bulgaria, 2015. *The National Strategy in the Area of Migration, Asylum and Integration 2015–2020.* [Online] Available at: https://www.strategy.bg/StrategicDocuments/View.aspx?lang=bg-BG&Id=963 [Accessed 3 March 2021].

Council of Ministers of the Republic Bulgaria, 2021. *National Migration Strategy of the Republic of Bulgaria 2021–2025.* [Online] Available at: https://mvr.bg/docs/default-source/strategicheskidokumenti/национална-стратегия-по-миграция-на-република-българия-2021---2025-г.pdf?sfvrsn=c2951dba_2 [Accessed 15 May 2021].

Council of Ministers of the Republic of Bulgaria, 2008. *National Strategy on Migration and Integration 2008–2015.* [Online] Available at: https://www.strategy.bg/StrategicDocuments/View.aspx?lang=bg-BG&Id=462 [Accessed 3 March 2021].

Council of Ministers of the Republic of Bulgaria, 2018, January 30. *Săvmestna deklaratsiya na ministăr-predsedatelya na Republika Bălgariya g-n Plamen Oresharski i na Prezidenta na Republika Bălgariya g-n Rosen Plevneliev.* [Online] Available at: http://old.government.bg/cgi-bin/e-cms/vis/vis.pl?s=001&p=0213&n=560&g=

Dodov, S., 2015. Razkazi za bejanskata kriza. In *Ubejni Tochki.* Sofia: Diversia.

European Commission, 2019. *Bulgaria Establishes National Council on Migration, Borders, Asylum and Integration.* [Online] Available at: https://ec.europa.eu/migrant-integration/news/bulgaria-establishes-national-council-on-migration-borders-asylum-and-integration

European Commission, 2021. *Bulgaria: Twice as Many Receive Bulgarian Citizenship Compared to 2019.* [Online] Available at: https://ec.europa.eu/migrant-integration/news/bulgaria-twice-as-many-receive-bulgarian-citizenship-compared-to-2019

European Economic and Social Council, 2019. *Misson Report – Bulgaria.* s.l.: s.n.

Geddes, A. and Scholten, P., 2016. *The Politics of Migration & Immigration in Europe.* Los Angeles: Sage.

Hristova, T., Apostolova, R., Deneva, N. and Fiedle, M., 2014. *TRAPPED IN EUROPE'S QUAGMIRE: The Situation of Asylum Seekers and Refugees in Bulgaria.* s.l.: Border monitoring.eu.

Krasteva, A., Staykova, E., and Otova, I., 2011. *Satisfying Labor Demand Through Migration in Bulgaria 2004 – 2009.* Sofia: European Migration Network.

Krasteva, A., 2013. Bulgarian migration profile. [Online] Available at: https:// annakrasteva.wordpress.com/2013/03/21/bulgarian-migration-profile/ [Accessed 8 March 2021].

Krasteva, A., 2014. *Ot migratsia kum mobilnost. Politiki i putishta.* Sofia: New Bulgarian University.

Krasteva, A., 2018. *Hyperpoliticisation of Asylum and Responsibility: The Bulgarian Case: From Polarisation to Hegemonisation.* s.l.: CEASEVAL Project.

Krasteva, A., 2019. *The Bulgarian Migration Paradox. Migration and Development in Bulgaria.* Sofia: Caritas.

Markova, E., 2010. Optimising migration effects: A perspective from Bulgaria. In: R. B. Panţîru, ed. *A Continent Moving West?: EU Enlargement and Labour Migration from Central and Eastern Europe.* Amsterdam: Amsterdam University Press, pp. 207–230.

Ministry of Labour and Social Policy. 2004. 'East-West Migration in an Enlarged Europe'. Report prepared for the Conference 'Migration: Trends and Policies', organised by ICMPD Vienna and the Open Society Institute-Sofia, Sofia, [Accessed 9–10 December 2004].

MIPEX, 2020. *Key Findings. Bulgaria.* [Online] Available at: https://www.mipex. eu/bulgaria [Accessed 11 December 2020].

Mondon, A. W., 2020. *Reactionary Democracy: How Racism and the Populist Far Right Became Mainstream.* London: Verso.

National Assembly, 2018a, July 20. *Minute Records of the National Assembly.* [Online] Available at: https://www.parliament.bg/bg/plenaryst

National Assembly, 2018b, July 13/20. *National Assembly Protocol.* [Online] Available at: https://www.parliament.bg/bg/plenaryst

Nedeva, D., 2017. *State of Preparedness of the Republic of Bulgaria for Joining the Schengen Zone.* [Online] Available at: https://osis.bg/wp-content/uploads/2018/04/OSI_Publication_EU_11_en.pdf [Accessed 12 March 2021].

Otova, I. S., 2017. *Bulgaria. Country Report.* s.l.: CEASEVAL Project.

Vankova, Z. and Draganov, D., 2020. Migrants' access to social protection in Bulgaria. In: D. Vintila and J. M. Lafleur, ed. *Migration and Social Protection in Europe and Beyond* (Vol. 1). s.l.: IMISCOE Research Series. Springer, pp. 65–80.

Vankova, Z., Ilareva, V. and Bechev, D., 2017. Bulgaria, the EU and the 'Refugee Crisis. How to Improve the Policies on International Protection and Refugee Integration?. [Online] Available at: http://eupolicy.eu/wp-content/uploads/2017/04/doklad_bejanci_final.pdf

Wilde, P. d., 2011. No polity for old politics? A framework for analyzing the politicization of European integration. *Journal of European Integration*, 33(5), pp. 559–575.

Wilde, P. d., 2016. Introduction: The differentiated politicization of European governance. *West European Politics*, 39(1), pp. 3–22.

Zolberg, A., 1989. The next waves: Migration theory for a changing world. *International Migration Review*, 23(3), pp. 403–430.

3   Refugees in Bulgaria after 1989

Statistical reality and institutionalisation of the phenomenon

In the preceding chapter we took an opportunity to say that Bulgaria recognised migration as an issue of political order only too late and that the topic has remained marginal to the society for years into the period of democratic changes which started in 1989. In the present section we shall concentrate on the refugee phenomenon. It represents the earliest institutionalised type of migration in Bulgaria. The exception, however, rather confirms the rule. The reasons for this fact relate precisely to the process of democratisation, which envisages also harmonisation of legislation and its enforcement practices in Bulgaria with international legal standards in the area of human rights, including with regard to asylum granting: "After 1989, the Bulgarian policy for asylum and refugees was reformulated in accordance with the pro-Western course adopted by the country, and the national legislation was harmonized with the principles of international law" (Nakova & Erolova, 2019, p. 428). This trend is intensified in the process of preparation for EU membership and its actual implementation:

> Since 1995, when Bulgaria applied for membership in the European Union, the country began to follow the common European policy in the field of asylum and refugees and, respectively, began to bring national laws [into] harmony with European legislation; after 2007, when the country acceded to the EU, it was obliged to obey this legislation.
>
> (idem.)

This book begins with the 1989 transition, which to a great extent accounts for the migration panorama, and the second great transition is associated with the location of Bulgaria on the Balkan Refugee Route. Using this moment as a divider in the processes, in the following chapters we shall examine the institutionalisation of the refugee

DOI: 10.4324/9781003161493-4

phenomenon in Bulgaria. It is a kind of case study, reinforcing the tendency described in the previous chapter – the more politics is in evidence, the less policies are being made.

Where there are no refugees, there are institutions

Asylum was the first and best institutionalised area of the migration phenomenon in the initial years of the post-1989 democratic transition even though the number of asylum seekers prior to the 2015 refugee crisis was insignificant.

The dynamics of the refugee phenomenon might be set out in two directions: one is purely statistical and pertains to the quantitative dimensions of the phenomenon – the number of asylum seekers. The second involves the institutionalisation of the refugee phenomenon.

Before the year 2000, numbers vacillated between 250 and 1000. There was certain rise in the numbers around 1999–2000, which to a certain extent can be attributable by the events in Kosovo. The fact that the politicisation of the migration topic is of interest to our analysis warrants saying that the Kosovo crisis had acquired certain political dimension in Bulgaria (OMDA, 1999). There is no actual debate on whether or not refugees should be received, with the politicians of Bulgaria demonstrating a praiseworthy consensus on the subject. There are also some tentative tendencies which later found their way into the earliest documents concerning migration and into the political discourse on the subject: primordialism, seen in the emphasis laid on the migrants with Bulgarian origin, and welfare nationalism, surfacing and the line of opposition migrants – Bulgarians. The subject retained relevance for the time being, although mainly in the periphery of the intense confrontation between government and opposition concerning the position of the country on the military intervention in Kosovo. In spite of several bombastic media headlines, no broad public debate ensued.

Returning to figures, a relative apex is seen to ensue in 2002, with the submission of 2,888 asylum applications – ten times the number of applications submitted in 1993, when keeping of statistics had commenced. Even back then, the scale of the refugee flow was neither perceived as menacing nor was it seen to exceed the capacity of available institutional infrastructure capacitated to handle refugees in Bulgaria. There were numerous forecasts predicting that Bulgaria would attract huge waves of refugees following the country's 2007 accession to the EU. This development failed to materialise in the years 2007–2010 with numbers for the period remaining below 1,000 (Figure 3.1).

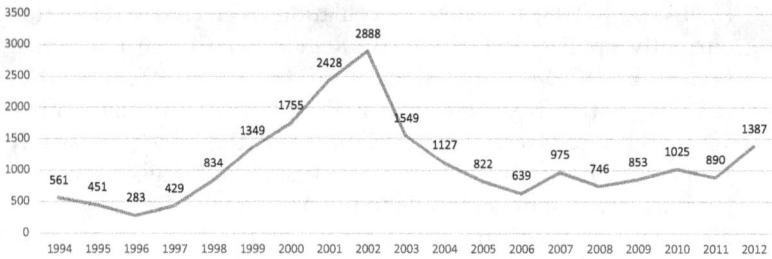

Figure 3.1 Asylum applicants 1993–2012.
Source: The authors, after data provided by SAR: http://www.aref.government.bg/
index.php/bg/aktualna-informacia-i-spravki

The second issue under scrutiny is the institutionalisation of the phenomenon. Upon signing the Geneva Convention in 1993, Bulgaria joined the family of asylum-granting countries. Bulgaria has also signed the New York Protocol thus undertaking the commitment to accept asylum-seeking foreigners without enforcement of any geographical or chronological limitations on the individuals in question (Nakova, 2019). The *non-refoulement* principle was enacted into Bulgarian legislation with Decree No. 208 / 4 October 1994 on Granting and Regulating Refugee Status, adopted by the Council of Ministers. Having started the application process for EU membership, Bulgaria gradually harmonised its legislation with European frameworks in the domain of asylum granting. As of the end of the 1990s, the national policy in the area of asylum granting was not regulated by a legal act, being governed instead by regulations and decrees issued in compliance with adopted / ratified international conventions and in cooperation with international and European organisations (Nakova, 2019). In 1999, the 38 National Assembly of the Republic of Bulgaria passed the Law on Refugees, and in 2002, the 39 National Assembly produced the Asylum and Refugees Act, with several amendments to it voted later (2005, 2006, 2007, 2009, 2011, 2013, 2014, 2015, and 2016). After 2007, when it had acceded to the EU, Bulgaria practically became a member of the Common European Asylum System (CEAS):

The main aim of the system is to develop common standards for equal treatment of persons seeking asylum in the EU; in connection with this, the EU developed and adopted a number of normative instruments including: the Lisbon Treaty (signed in 2007, in effect since 2009), the European Pact on Immigration and Asylum (EPIA) (13440/08), the Dublin Regulation I, II и III (the regulation currently applied is Dublin III, Regulation EU 604/2013), the system EURODAC (EU Regulation No. 407/2002), DubliNet (EU Regulation No. 1560/2003), EUROSUR (EU Regulation No. 1052/2013) etc. Overall, the Parliament of Bulgaria successfully transposed European directives into Bulgarian legislation, and [continual] amendments made to the Asylum and Refugee Act of 2002 indicate that legislators were striving to [conform] current resolutions of European legislation into the CEAS framework.

(Nakova, 2019)

Protection comes in several types. Asylum is one type of protection granted to foreigners persecuted for reason of their convictions or activities in defence of internationally recognised rights and freedoms. It is granted by the (Vice) President of the Republic of Bulgaria in conformity to Art. 98 (10) of the Constitution of the Republic of Bulgaria. International protection incorporates refugee status and humanitarian status pursuant to Art. 1 (2) of the Law on Asylum and Refugees and is granted by the Chairperson of the State Agency for Refugees in conformity with Art. 2 (3) of the Law on Asylum and Refugees. Temporary protection shall be granted in the event of a mass influx of foreigners forced to leave their country of origin due to a military conflict, civil war, foreign aggression, violation of human rights, or indiscriminate violence on the territory of the relevant country or in a part of the country, and who for these reasons are unable to return thereto (Law on Asylum and Refugees, Art. 1 (3) by the Council of Ministers). This instrument has never been applied. The fourth type is the asylum. In fact, although it exists as an instrument, and there is a special commission attached to the Vice-President, asylum is almost never granted. Practically, there are no accessible public data on the asylum-granting procedure. Sporadic data providing some approximate pictures are available:

For the period between 22 January 2002 and 21 January 2012, there were submitted applications for granting of asylum in Bulgaria by 159 people, nationals of 36 states. For the indicated period asylum was not granted to: 127 people – due to evident lack of grounds for the submission and/or misuse of the right to asylum, including with the purpose of thwarting the enforcement of compulsory administrative measures enforced against them; 13 people who had obtained humanitarian status from the State Agency of Refugees at the Council of Ministers, had received a permit for permanent residence, or had left permanently the territory of the Republic of Bulgaria during active asylum-granting proceedings; and 4 people to whom the Vice President of the Republic of Bulgaria has denied issuing an asylum decree in rejection to the proposal to issue a decree made by the Commission for Granting Asylum. The proceedings on 9 cases, which commenced in the period specified, have been terminated. Resolution was adjourned until after 21 January 2012 for 6 correspondence dossiers on applications submitted for asylum in the Republic of Bulgaria.

(President of the Republic of Bulgaria, 2012)

According to the Asylum and Refugees Act and in conformity to international and European norms, any foreign national can request international protection in the Republic of Bulgaria. While the protection-granting procedure is in progress, and after obtaining protection, the foreign national shall not be returned to the territory of a country where his/her life or freedom is endangered for reason of his/her race, religion, nationality, membership of a specific social group or political persuasion, or where he/she faces a threat of torture or other forms of cruel, inhuman, or degrading treatment or punishment. The foreigners who have lodged an application for asylum or have obtained asylum in the country shall bear civil, administrative criminal and criminal liability under the terms and procedures applicable to Bulgarian nationals. For the duration of the procedure for granting asylum, the applicants shall have all the rights and obligations provided by the Law on Asylum and Refugees. On the grounds of Art. 31 in conjunction with Art. 32 (1), item 1–4 of the Law on Asylum and Refugees, a foreigner who has been granted asylum shall have the rights and obligations of a Bulgarian citizen, except for:

- the right to participate in general and municipal elections, in national and regional referenda, to take part in the founding of political parties and to become a member to such parties;
- the right to hold positions for which the law requires to have to have Bulgarian citizenship;
- the right to serve in the army;
- other restrictions explicitly provided for by the law (Law on Asylum and Refugees).

As early as 1992, the National Office on Territorial Asylum and Refugees was established at the Council of Ministers under Decree No.

207/23 (1992) of the Council of Ministers. In 2000, the Office was upgraded into an Agency of the Refugees and as of 2002, the State Agency for Refugees under the Council of Ministers is designated as the government institution tasked with matters pertaining to the refugee phenomenon:

> In the course of its restructurings, it has always been the main body responsible for implementation of national legislation (laws and decrees) on asylum and refugees. Its work is assisted by [other government bodies] such as the Ministry of the Interior, the Ministry of Foreign Affairs, the State Agency for National Security, the Ministry of Labor and Social Policy, the Ministry of Education and Science, and by various non-government organizations.
>
> (Nakova and Erolova, 2019 p. 429)

It incorporates operative centres where asylum seekers reside during the examination procedure of their application. In 1997, the first centre for registration and reception of asylum seekers and refugees opened in the village of Banya, while 2001 saw the opening of the registration and reception centre in the Ovcha Kupel district of Sofia, followed by the Pastrogor transit centre in the municipality of Svilengrad, southern Bulgaria, in 2008. It is evident that until this moment all government actions are subject to enactment of synchronisation of the legislative base and practice with the international legal standards enshrined in the Geneva Convention and the New York Protocol.

Prior to 2012–2013, the reception system was stable and was of little interest other than to a few international and national humanitarian organisations (Staykova and Otova, 2019). December 2005 saw adopted the first National Program for Refugee Integration in the Republic of Bulgaria (2005–2007), which became operative in practice in 2006. In 2008 there was adopted a follow-up / subsequent document with duration of validity / temporal scope until 2010, followed up by a third document for the period 2011–2013. As summarised by Ilareva:

> Between 2005 and 2013, SAR was implementing refugee integration based on the National Program for Integration of Refugees in the Republic of Bulgaria with a three-year programming period. This document containing steps for the practical enforcement of European legal standards and the integration of asylum recipients

into society became another basis for coordinating the actions of the institutions and the nongovernment organizations. Between 23 and 60 people annually were entitled to integrational support up to one year from receiving international protection. The support included financial assistance for housing, social assistance, health insurance, Bulgarian language training, social orientation and cultural adaptation, vocational training, translation services and cooperation in the realization / consummation of their basic rights.

(Vankova et al., 2017)

Albena Tcholakova notes that there are also certain inclusion measures laid down in other documents, such as the Literacy Program for Literacy, Qualification and Employment of Recipients of Refugee or Humanitarian Status from 2004, adopted by the Ministry of Labor and Social Policy. However, it covers no more than 40 people solely from Sofia and the adjacent region (Tcholakova, 2012, p. 174). Tcholakova also emphasises the significant role of international organisations, such as UNHCR and the non-governmental sector in enforcing and implementing the measures as well as regarding the overall establishment of the admission system in Bulgaria. Thus, for example, as early as 1997, using funding from UNHCR, was established the Centre for Integration of Refugee Women, which was reorganised in 2001 with a Resolution of the Council of Ministers as the Centre for Integration at State Agency for Refugees (SAR) (Tcholakova, 2012, p. 178).

Thus, with an insignificant number of protection seekers and status recipients, the state, although mainly for the sake of its international partners, possessed a less or more efficient system for international protection and reception of protection seekers and refugees. The topic remained outside the view of the society and politicians of Bulgaria, with an only exception which was already mentioned. The dynamics of the changes in reception system policies in the 1990s were not directly associated with the prevailing number of asylum seekers and migration flows but were related to the overall process of the democratisation of Bulgarian society and institutions; and, at a later stage, also the process of EU accession. Nevertheless, due to a lack of planning and several other institutional setbacks, crystallising in the process of the rather formal utilisation of European funds and the apparent synchronisation of statutory acts and practices rather than in an essential upgrading of management capacity and investment in a stable system, the post-2012 situation found Bulgaria completely unprepared.

Where there are refugees, there are no working institutions

What happened, however, after Bulgaria found itself located on the Balkan Refugee Route?

The rise in the figures began after the number of asylum applications increased six times from 1,387 in 2012 to 7,144 in 2013. The peak occurred in 2015, which saw 20,391 people apply for asylum – an unprecedented number for Bulgaria. The following 2016 year was marked by a halt in the increase and even a slight decline in the number of asylum seekers – a total of 19,418 applications, although numbers remained much higher than prior to the peak – 11,081 in 2014 (Figure 3.2).

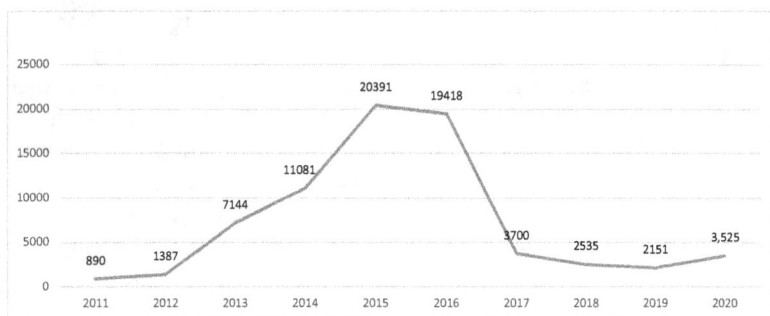

Figure 3.2 Asylum application 2011–2020.
Source: The authors, after data provided by SAR: http://www.aref.government.bg/index.php/bg/aktualna-informacia-i-spravki

As a result of this peak in the number of asylum applications, new arrivals to the country had to face a situation of institutional collapse, political and media ostracism and growing social tensions (Staykova and Otova, 2019). After 2015, the migration phenomenon was completely dominated by pressure from waves of the so-called "mixed migration", encountered by the EU, part of which passed through the territory of Bulgaria. Although there were moments of institutional "suffocation" for a short period of time, as we shall see in a while, the overcrowded accommodation centres were quickly emptied. Most of the people which had made an entry into the country continued their way onward to Central and Western Europe. This type of migration transit was to certain extent facilitated by the political will and by the lack of "amiable humanitarian approach".

The government of Bulgaria adopted a plan in response to mounting migratory pressures on 16 April 2014 – almost a year after the actual onset of the crisis. In this connection, the incumbent Deputy Prime Minister and Minister of the Interior, Tsvetlin Yovchev, commented as follows:

We have reckoned with the deteriorating situation in Afghanistan and the Middle East. It is understood that refugee accommodation facilities in locations nearby to Syria would have exceeded their capacity by now and it falls to our country to face once again heightened migratory pressures. This risk is [considered] currently [a matter] of no urgent actuality but eventually, and within a few upcoming months, it may happen. It is because of this [eventuality] that we must be in readiness.

He further announced that no new camps were projected for construction, but that the government planned to obviate another crisis by securing new beds for existing facilities: "This buffer is to be installed at the accommodation locations, although not presently" (Monitor, 2014). We should remind ourselves that what was estimated by the government to be no urgent risk had materialised into 20,391 asylum applications in 2015, nearly twice the number of the preceding year.

By early 2013, the total capacity of the reception centres comprised 805 places, grouped as follows: 425 places in the Sofia facility; 80 in the reception centre of Banya, central Bulgaria; and 300 at the Pastrogor transit centre in the border area with Turkey and Greece (AIDA, 2013). This overall capacity proved rather insufficient with the numbers of arriving asylum seekers on the increase well past mid-2013 (AIDA, 2013). To cope with the situation, the State Agency for Refugees opened new accommodation facilities, more particularly several so-called "provisional accommodation centres" in the Vrazhdebna district of Sofia in September 2013 and, a few weeks later, in the capital's Voenna Rampa district. The capacity of the former allowed the housing of 420 with the latter housing 500. None of these facilities were designed to serve these designated purposes and living conditions were the subject of criticism from human rights organisations. Because of the conditions in asylum seeker reception facilities, which had sparked protests across immigrant communities, the Bulgarian Helsinki Committee (BHC) even demanded the resignation of the government. The BHC classifies this crisis as an instance of radical institutionalised arrogation of fundamental human. Meanwhile, a third centre for temporary accommodation opened in Harmanli using the facilities of a former military base with the capacity to house 450 people. Asylum Information Database (AIDA) has reported even worse on-location conditions "with asylum seekers placed in a confinement regime and accommodated in tents and 'containers' lacking electricity and sewerage, under extremely poor living and hygienic conditions and at the heightened risk of epidemics" (Savova, 2013). Criticism of the treatment of asylum seekers was also expressed in a Human Rights Watch report announced in Sofia in April 2014. The incumbent Interior Minister, Tsvetlin Yovchev, qualified the allegations as "outright falsehoods and libels against Bulgaria," while the director of the State Agency for Refugees, Nikolay Chirpanliev, described the organisation as "a bunch of morons, liars and swindlers, misleading public opinion in an impudent, cynical and dishonest way" (Capital Daily, 2014).

In subsequent years, living conditions in reception facilities have gradually reached acceptable standards, mainly with support from European funds and from donations by international organisations. In August 2016, however, a mass brawl broke out between Afghani and Iraqi asylum seekers at the Harmanli centre. On 24 November, provisional restrictions placed on free movement in and out of the same centre generated further riots on the premises of the institution. In the weeks preceding this incident, rumours had been afloat in the community that there was an outbreak of infectious disease at the centre. Despite the repeated reassurance of the authorities that the situation was not epidemiologically dangerous or capable of affecting employees in the centre or town residents, and that it involved standard cases of chickenpox, a disease typical in Bulgaria, Harmanli residents demanded that the authorities enforce medical examinations on the premises and that the media should attend them. Organised protests entailed the enforcement of provisional measures restricting uninhibited exiting of inmates from facility grounds. The riots resulted in 400 Afghan and Iraqi nationals being placed under detention, 1,000 people being removed from the facility and 24 police officers injured. The riot was followed by the appointment of a new director and further reorganisations implemented at the establishment. Afterwards, all centres across Bulgaria started to implement the ethnic principle of accommodation (Staykova and Otova, 2019).

Detention centres in Bulgaria (located at Busmantsi, Lyubimets, and Elhovo[1]) are under the administration of the Migration Directorate of the Ministry of Interior. After 2016, a new provision allowed for asylum seekers to be placed in closed reception facilities under the jurisdiction of the State Agency for Refugees while the handling of their applications is in progress. This legislative amendment also accounts for the Harmanli riots and the reactions of several political actors.

In September 2017, the government introduced so-called 'statutory movement zones' comprising the geographical environs surrounding any given reception centre. Asylum seekers may request a permission to leave the zone and in case the request is rejected, the motive for the rejection must be stated as well. Permission is not required in cases where asylum seekers must leave the zone to report before a court or another public authority, or if they need emergency medical assistance (Staykova and Otova, 2019).

Three registration and reception centres were operating as of 2018, with these being used for registration, accommodation, and the conduct of procedures in the interior of the country. These include:

- Harmanli registration and reception centre;
- Banya registration and reception centre;
- Sofia registration and reception centre, with three sub-divisions located in the districts of Ovcha Kupel, Vrazhdebna and Voenna Rampa.

Following the November 2016 riots at Harmanli, the authorities began to accommodate individuals from different nationalities in different facilities: Voenna Rampa is inhabited by Afghan and Pakistani asylum seekers, as well as single Iraqis; Ovcha Kupel houses mainly families from Syria, Iraq and Africa; as well as exceptions, such as nationals of Myanmar; the occupants of Vrazhdebna are also single Syrian nationals and there are no families there. Asylum seekers accommodated at Harmanli must be allocated according to ethnicity or nationality principles.

Authorities began to escort asylum seekers coming to Sofia from Harmanli back to their original accommodation location. According to a statement made by a SAR operative, refugees prefer Sofia as a place of residence because it is seen to afford better chances to contact traffickers who might assist their departure from the country rather than any essential differences in handling asylum seekers between the two locations. In compliance with the system of statutory movement zones in force, asylum seekers are allowed to move freely anywhere in Sofia but, if they are apprehended a second time outside their zone without permission, and where a record of the infringement is drawn up, the authorities are empowered to return them to a confined centre. A new closed type of centre installed by the SAR, with capacity to accommodate 60 people, is already operational in Sofia. Whereas the initial collapse of the reception system prompted the opening of more accommodation centres, but with almost no essential changes effected in procedural management, the Harmanli incidents led to no fewer than three innovations: the ethnic principle of accommodating asylum seekers in view of avoiding conflicts between different nationalities; the possibilities of establishing closed-type centres under the jurisdiction of the SAR after 2016; and the enforcement[2] after 2017 of so-called statutory movement zones restricting the right of movement for asylum seekers within limited geographic boundaries. Such measures were adopted on an ad hoc and post-event basis; and rather than effecting essential changes in the governance of the reception system, they were devised to surmount recurrent tensions and satisfy public expectations which were aroused not without the participation of various political actors and media, rather than launching effective policies and instituting a stable system.

The number of migrants traditionally experienced by Bulgaria is much lower than the experience in neighbouring Greece, to cite an example. It is a long-standing practice of authorities in Bulgaria to deny Turkish nationals access to international protection procedures and repatriate them, including occasional cases of violation of the non-refoulement principle. In return, Turkish authorities divert a large part of migration pressure from Bulgaria to the borders of Greece. The most recent instance of this practice was the border crisis from March 2020 in the area of Pazarkule-Kastanies border point, with almost no attempts being made to enter Bulgaria. Nevertheless, a significant number of asylum applicants continue to attempt entry into the EU via Bulgaria. In 2020, authorities have issued 4,658 formal denials of passage and allegedly carried out 498 acts of indirect repulsion which affected 3,493 people, as well as 569 acts of direct repulsion affecting another 11,770, as indicated by the national border monitoring (Savova, 2020).

Large numbers of third-country nationals continued to transit and exit the country without any interference from national authorities. Most detained individuals later escaped when released upon submitting and registering asylum applications. Although there was a reduction in these figures in 2020 on account of the COVID crisis, they still account for 83% of the total number of the asylum-seeking people in the country. The Western Balkans became the most active migration route in 2020 as figures doubled in comparison with those from the end of 2019. This is also due to a significant decrease of the illegal crossings at the EU's external borders along the Eastern, Central and Western Mediterranean routes (Savova, 2020).

An interesting observation of statistics on Bulgaria also indicates that in 2020 the number of people seeking international protection in Bulgaria has risen to the levels from 2017. The number of new arrivals has increased by 57% compared to 2019. This fact, apart from being a modest confirmation that crises, regardless of their character – be it military, medical, or financial, only become superimposed on each other and do not put a stop to migration – breeds serious misgivings linked to the complication of the humanitarian dimensions of the refugee phenomenon. Data indicate that the pandemic has affected different groups unevenly, with refugees and protection seekers belonging to the most vulnerable.

As mentioned above, during the Covid-19 pandemic the applications for asylum in the country did not cease. On the contrary, there was certain increase of their number as compared to the previous year. It is noteworthy that in 2020 the institutions involved in the process have reported only 131 integration profiles of foreigners who have stated their interest for permanent settlement in the country.

Prior to the crises, Bulgaria's National Program for Integration of Refugees had functioned well. We need to remind that the next National Program was devised to cover the period 2011–2013, however, the State Agency for the Refugees surprisingly failed to renew the programme for the next period despite the increase in refugee arrivals. This provides grounds for criticism from local and international organisations. The Council of Europe, for instance, stresses:

According to the Law on Asylum, refugees and beneficiaries of subsidiary protection should have access to integration programs on housing, employment and health care. In practice, however, the integration opportunities for refugees and beneficiaries of subsidiary protection in Bulgaria are rather scarce.

(Council of Europe, 2018)

While the Bulgarian Helsinki Committee wrote:

The National Program for Integration of Refugees was in force until the end of 2013, but since then all beneficiaries of international protection have [remained] almost entirely without integration support. This resulted in extremely limited access or ability by these individuals to enjoy even the most basic social, labor and health rights.

(Bulgarian Helsinki Committee, 2019)

An appendage to the adopted in 2015 National Strategy in the area of migration, asylum and integration, which is referred to in the previous chapter, a National Action Plan on the integration of refugees is projected for development, but it also failed to become a reality (Vankova et al., 2017). In August 2016, the government adopted an Ordinance for the Integration Agreement in relation to the execution of the Asylum and Refugee Act, according to the leading role in the integration process to local communities / municipalities (Vankova et al., 2017). However, the document has remained in disuse for 2016 and 2017, as no local municipalities had applied for the financial subsidy necessary to initiate the integration procedures with the foreign nationals who were granted international protection in Bulgaria (Bulgarian Helsinki Committee, 2019). A new Decree was adopted in 2017, which essentially repeated the provisions of the former. Since its adoption, only 13 status recipients have benefitted from integration support, but all of them were relocated with integration funding provided under the EU relocation scheme, not by the general national integration mechanism (Bulgarian Helsinki Committee, 2019). Even the decentralization of the responsibilities for immigration from the government to local municipalities would in principle be a sensible step forward, [if not for] the fact that the discharge of such responsibilities is actually not prescribed as mandatory but left to the discretion of municipalities, which has called to question the effectiveness of the measures [taken to effect] integration in Bulgaria. This was illustrated by fact that no municipality has volunteered to conclude Integration Agreements, although funds would be allocated to them for every refugee participating in such agreements (Council of Europe, 2018).

The example with the adopted decree is extremely emblematic of how a policy fails to start working in practice on account of political discourse and attitudes generated in society, which we shall revisit in the next chapter to analyse in detail.

Resulting from peaking numbers in asylum applications, new arrivals in the country were confronted by a situation of institutional collapse, political and media ostracism and mounting social tensions. Accommodation centres were unavailable, and in what were available the conditions were unacceptable. No working mechanisms for handling applications were in place, neither was there such as can ensure the bare minimum of standards to safeguard the protection of human rights. Despite ostensible normalisation of the situation in subsequent years, the reception system has failed to undergo significant changes on account of the crisis. Normalisation can be attributed to factors extraneous to the system, and the few changes to be affected came in response to the dominant securitarian reading and anti-immigrant sentiment. The erected obstacles – the wire-fencing installation on the border, which was referred to in the former chapter – and suspended integration programmes clearly outline two trends in Bulgaria's policies towards seekers of protection and refugees – the unwillingness to have them allowed on the national territory and the unwillingness to admit them into the community. Nevena Nancheva has summarised this process:

> The analysis of Bulgaria's response to the refugee influx of 2013–14, offered below, demonstrates two things. First, security thinking and acts of securitization (Huysmans, 2006, p. 149) have completely overhauled the human right aspects of asylum, institutionalizing a peculiar European Union predicament: policies that aim at protection from asylum seekers, rather than at protection of asylum seekers. Second, these policies reinforce a very visible exclusion of asylum seekers from participation in the political community of the state, spelling a recipe for xenophobia, racism and segregation, with all their concomitant evils that the European Union has been proclaiming to combat.
>
> (Nancheva, 2016)

Responsible in a significant extent got this state of affairs, apart from the policies themselves, were some narratives about migration and in particular those about the seekers of protection and refugees, which have taken shape through the political discourse and the media in order to create steady symbolic universes. Societal attitudes provide an ample proof for this: in a national representative research by the Bulgarian Academy of Sciences (2019) to the question

> "Do you think that Bulgaria must receive refugees?"[3] 64,1% of the respondents have answered in the negative, namely "No, Bulgaria should not receive refugees". The motives of this group of individuals under scrutiny relate to reasons such as: the state has no financial ability to meet the expenses for their sustenance (20,9%); because some of them might be people who can pose a threat to the national security of the country (20,7%); because there is the possibility of civil conflicts erupting in the locations where they have settled (13,5%); because they are carriers of other culture, quite different from ours (9,0%).
>
> (Nakova, 2019, p. 276)

Notes

1 Inoperative as of 2017.
2 Until that point, closed-type centres operated only under the jurisdiction of the Direction of Migration at the Ministry of the Interior.
3 Nakova has made the important specification that in the mentality of Bulgarians, a refugee is a generalised, cumulative embodiment of all migrants, coming from "precarious regions" (Nakova, 2019: BAS Demographic).

Bibliography

AIDA, 2013. *Annual Report 2012/2013*. [Online] Available at: from Asylum Information Database: https://asylumineurope.org/annual-report-20122013/ [Accessed 2 February 2021].

Bulgarian Helsinki Committee, 2019. *2019 as the Sixth "Zero Integration Year"*. [Online] Available at: https://www.asylumineurope.org/reports/country/bulgaria/content-international-protection/2019-sixth-%E2%80%9Czero-integration-year%E2%80%9D [Accessed 11 December 2020.].

Capital Daily, 2014, April 30. Capital Daily. s.l.: s.n.

Council of Europe, 2018). *Report of the Fact-finding Mission by Ambassador Tomáš Boček, Special Representative of the Secretary General on Migration and Refugees to Bulgaria, SG/Inf(2018)18*. [Online] Available at: https://rm.coe.int/report-of-the-fact-finding-mission-by-ambassador-tomas-bocek-special-r/16807be041 [Accessed 11 December 2020].

Huysmans, J., 2006. *The Politics of Insecurity: Fear, Migration and Asylum in the EU* (Vol. New International Relations Series.). London: Routledge.

Milcheva, E., 2013. *Ne e 1999, Kostov go niama, a idvat bejancite*. [Online] Available at: https://webcafe.bg/vlast/562213042-ne-e-1999-kostov-go-nyama-a-bezhantsite-idvat.html [Accessed 6 March 2021].

Monitor, 2014. *https://www.monitor.bg*. [Online] Available at: https://www.monitor.bg: https://www.monitor.bg/bg/search/2014 [Accessed 7 March 2021].

Nakova, A., 2019. Predstavi i naglasi na bŭlgarskite grazhdani kŭm bezhantsite i tyakhnoto znachenie za uspeshnoto realizirane na natsionalnata politika v oblastta na mezhdunarodnata zakrila. In *Migration and National Identity*. Sofia: BAN.

Nakova, A. and Erolova, Y., 2019. Integration by 'Fencing': The Case of Refugees in Bulgaria. In: M. Slavkova, M. Maeva, Y. Erolova, and R. Popov eds. *Between the Worlds: People, Spaces and Rituals*, Sofia: IEFSEM – BAS & Paradigma, 425–453.

Nancheva, N., 2016. Bulgaria's response to refugee migration: Institutionalizing the boundary of exclusion. *Journal of Refugee Studies*, 29(4), pp. 549–567.

OMDA, 1999. *Pregled na pechata*. [Online] Available at: omda.bg: http://www.omda.bg/public/bulg/news/release/050499.HTM [Accessed 6 March 2021].

President of the Republic of Bulgaria, 2012. *Report for the Period from 22.01.2002 to 21.01.2012*. [Online] Available at: https://www.president.bg/docs/1351451646.pdf [Accessed 5 March 2021].

Savova, I., 2013, November 25. *National Country Report*. [Online] Available at: https://asylumineurope.org/wp-content/uploads/2015/08/report-download_aida_bulgaria_report_-_first_update_-_final.pdf [Accessed 2 February 2021].

Savova, I., 2020. *Country Report: Bulgaria*. s.l.: AIDA.

Staykova, E. and Otova, I., 2019. *When Politics Kill Policies. Mainstreaming Populism vs Solidarity Movments: Reception of Refugees in Bulgaria*. s.l.: CEASEVAL.

Tcholakova, A., 2012. *En quête de travail, enjeux de reconnaissance et remaniement identitaire : approche comparée France-Bulgarie de carrières professionnelles de réfugiés.* Sofia: NBU.

Vankova, Z., Ilareva, V. and Bechev, D., 2017. *Bulgaria, the EU and the 'Refugee Crisis. How to Improve the Policies on International Protection and Refugee Integration?.* [Online] Available at: http://eupolicy.eu/wp-content/uploads/2017/04/doklad_bejanci_final.pdf

4 Located on the Balkan Refugee Route amid rampant dominating populism – when politics kills policies

The present chapter is dedicated to the populist phenomenon in Bulgaria. In the first part, in a state-of-the art presentation of research by Bulgarian authors, we have outlined the basic trends, characteristic of the populist phenomenon in Bulgaria, at the same time tracing its chronological development until the point where it becomes a dominating phenomenon in the country's political process. Although it emerged at a late stage and at a moment when democracy in Bulgaria could already be described as consolidated, populism was apparently to remain on the political scene permanently. Although one can accept on principle the differentiation between populism and radical far-right, nationalism and nativism (Mudde, 2016; Pappas, 2019) we have chosen to use the former term due to the broader scope of the concept. The process of normalisation of populism in the example of Bulgaria makes these characteristics detectable with very few exceptions within all populist and populism-"infected" parties. This becomes particularly conspicuous through the example of migration. At the same time, we accept that this hypothesis would not have equal validity in different contexts, and we understand its limited character.

In the second part of the chapter, using migration and mostly migration crisis which found Bulgaria situated on the Balkan Refugee Route, and giving references to previous chapters, we investigate how populism, having become a norm, precludes policymaking and politics kill policies. Although the tendency of instrumentalising the "migrant" crisis is not symptomatic only of Bulgaria, the Bulgarian case has a lot of specifics which shall be analysed in order to find an answer to the question "actually, crisis of what is the crisis we are dealing with?"

DOI: 10.4324/9781003161493-5

Normalisation of populism

After the beginning of the twenty-first century, we have become witnesses to a new upsurge of the extremist parties and movements, of processes which have effectively "radicalized" the mainstream as well:

> Since the turn of the twenty-first century, radical right and radical left politics have entered into a new phase. Over the past decades, populist and radical actors have mobilized through electoral and protest channels and succeeded in radicalizing "mainstream" politics on the European continent and beyond. Whilst populist and radical parties have been responsible for the politicization of a number of issues (environmentalism, immigration, Euroscepticism, etc.), the issues at the core of their ideology are no longer exclusively owned by these organizations. Indeed, they have profoundly reshaped social and political cleavages at the national and supranational level
>
> (Gattinara, 2020)

In effect, this was a reversal which changed not just the political actors, but politics on the whole.

One thing should be made clear from the very beginning. There is, of course, a distinction between populism and (radical) extreme right (Mudde, 2016; Pappas, 2019). We have chosen to use the term populism precisely because of the wider scope of the concept, understanding it to a certain degree in the sense of Laclau's "empty signifier" (Medarov, 2017). We understand populism in terms of articulating political practices and not as a political object, or as written by Jansen "populism is not a 'thing' or 'object' to be studied but 'a mode of political practice'" (Jansen, 2011). Ivan Krastev also points out that it would not be entirely groundless to use the term "populism" as a generic term for political actors who differ between each other. In his opinion, only a fuzzy and poorly defined concept such as populism would allow us to comprehend and to explain the radical transformation in politics which is under way in many places across the world. The vague and loosely defined concept of "populism" allows us to grasp the nature of today's challenges faced by liberal democracy in a better way than any of the well-defined concepts which have currently entered widespread circulation would allow. These challenges do not come as a consequence of antidemocratic and authoritarian alternatives, but rather proceed from dangerous mutations inside liberal democracies themselves (Krastev, 2007). Ultimately, however, they may also lead to the former although in terms of genesis they happen within the latter.

The case of Bulgaria, as already mentioned, is not an exception, although it has some specifics of its own. We opted to introduce the topic through the state of the art of the work of Bulgarian researchers, as this will contextualise the reader better. As Ruth Wodak points out:

> When analyzing right-wing (or, indeed, left-wing) populist movements and their rhetoric, it is essential to recognize that their propaganda – realized as it is in many genres across relevant social domains – always combines and integrates form and content, targets specific audiences and adapts to specific contexts. Only by doing so we are able to deconstruct, understand and explain their messages, the resonance of their messages and their electoral success.
>
> (Wodak, 2015, p. 3)

In 2008, Daniel Smilov wrote: "Populism in Bulgaria already has some visible impact on Bulgarian politics: this is the 'mainstreaming' of nationalism" (Smilov, 2008, p. 38). In one of his texts from 2015 titled *The Bulgarian Radical Right. Marching Up from the Margins* Kiril Avramov emphasised: "The lack of a cordon sanitaire and the porosity between the mainstream and the margins has shifted the entire system into the right, and the tactics of 'taming' the 'marginals' actually produced a radicalization of the mainstream instead" (Avramov, 2015, p. 315). In the present study, we aim precisely at analysing this tendency of normalisation of (national)populism and its transformation into a norm in the political life of Bulgaria.

There seems to be certain consensus that populism has become the star-concept in Bulgarian political-science research since 2007 (Zhdrebev, 2019). One of the researchers who engaged in the conversation even wrote that the political debate in Bulgaria seems obsessed with the subject (Malinov, 2008). We will try to outline the main tendencies in it. A possible approach to the task might involve identifying cores within the Bulgarian debate around the tendency current in scientific literature around the world to talk about three possible approaches in understanding populism: as an ideology (ideational approach), as a discursive style (discursive-performative approach), or as a strategy for political mobilisation and movement (strategic approach) (Zhdrebev,

2019; Moffitt, 2020). Of course, in following this logic, we will try to stress much more on the specifics of the case under scrutiny, namely, the Bulgarian populist phenomenon.

Atanas Zhdrebev (Zhdrebev, 2019) has made one of the most conscientious reviews of scientific literature by Bulgarian authors who have researched the populist phenomenon. Along with others, he gives prominence to the work of several researchers: Smilov, who comes closest to the conception of populism as an ideological phenomenon; Malinov – endorsing its understanding as political rhetoric; and Karasimeonov and Andreev, treating the understanding of populism as a movement (Zhdrebev, 2019). Adopting his systematisation, we shall highlight only the details relevant to our analysis.

Smilov understands populism as "minimalist" ideology both in terms of content and internal coherence (Smilov, 2008), that is, it can be utilised by left- and right-wing parties alike. This interpretation is akin to Cas Mudde's conception of "thin ideology" (Mudde, 2004). In the Bulgarian context it is interesting to emphasise that the "co-existence" may occur both between parties, divided along the classical cleavage "right-left", and also along the axis, determining to a great extent the party system in the country in the early years of the transition – ex-communist vs. transition democrats: "thus, it is an attempt to transcend the established cleavages and divisions among 'mainstream' political parties, such as the 'left vs. right', or the 'ex–communists v. transition democrats" (Smilov, 2008, p. 15). This "adjustability" of populism is important from the perspective of our analysis, which investigates primarily its spread among political parties and movements of the entire spectrum and it's becoming a dominant element in the political process. This fits into the general behaviour trend of modern populism, which fails to pose a challenge to democracy in its capacity of system based on free elections and majority rule (Krastev, 2007). As shown by practice, however, they can certainly pose a challenge to liberalism:

> populism is democratic illiberalism: it is a political ideology and movement within liberal democracy, which threatens its constitutional, liberal foundations. As such populism has an anti-systemic agenda or at least creates a credible threat of being able to change important elements of liberal democracy.
>
> (Smilova, 2020)

In contrast to extremist parties of the 1930s, these populists do not seek prohibition of elections or establishment of dictatorships. On the contrary, they like elections, especially referenda, and unfortunately, often win them (Krastev, 2007). But at the same time:

> Populist strategies are highly partisan and self-serving: the opposition often becomes the enemy, which could be legitimately destroyed through the instruments of power. Thus, populism results in aggressive majoritarianism: it puts a lot of pressure on independent bodies (the judiciary, independent regulators, the media, etc.) and is skeptical of minority rights.
>
> (Smilova, 2020)

Malinov, who in contrast to Smilov understands populism as a "form of political thinking and talking, a set of rhetorical techniques with one leading characteristic – addressing and invoking the collective embodiment of the people against the elites" (Malinov, 2008), also emphasises what populism is not. Apart from not being an adequate ideology, as already clarified, Malinov reiterates the understanding that populism is neither left, nor right. Neither is it a sign of political immaturity. Malinov has found support for his thesis in the fact that populist "outbursts" are possible with new and established democracies alike (Malinov, 2008). Smilov talks about a "period of non–populist politics", using it to highlight one of the peculiarities of the Bulgarian populist phenomenon – its considerably late appearance (Smilov, 2008). Despite some examples which were in evidence as early as the first years after 1989, the star of Bulgarian populism rose on the Bulgarian political scene after 2001. The return to the country of the former king Simeon II marked the beginning of this new stage in the political life of the country and many researchers use this precise moment to build the chronological typology of the phenomenon in Bulgaria. Smilov suggests three waves: the first one is related to Simeon II and the sudden appearance of the National Movement Simeon the Second (NMSS), which won over 40% and half the seats in the National Assembly, the second relates to the appearance on the political scene of Volen Siderov and "Ataka" at the 2006 presidential elections, and the last one is the emergence of GERB and Boyko Borisov, who won in 2007 the elections for European Parliament. To these waves, later in the text we shall add another, which crystallised most saliently around the 2021 elections. Karasimeonov divided the post transitional[1] populism into two phases:

> The first is related to the depletion of confidence in the UDP due to disillusionment with the implemented reforms and with moral

and economic populism resting on the charisma of Simeon Saxe-Coburg-Gotha. The second phase is mainly related with the topics of nationalism and corruption, order and legality and along these lines, the party with pro-European orientation GERB assails MRF, while the anti-European party "Ataka" is driven by xenophobia and.

(Karasimeonov, 2008)

In fact, the very title of Karasimeonov's text reads "Does the Populism Concept Have Scientific Value?" What stands among the chief contributions of the article is precisely the uncertainty about the value of the term which can be perceived as difficult to formulate. Karasimeonov has also provided a definition of populism:

> ...populism, as a political movement in democratic context is based on mass popular discontent in a specific socially economic and political situation, exploiting anti-elitarist, including anti-party attitudes and suggests radical changes in the status-quo. Its political manifestation can be radical, anti-systemic or systemic within the framework of democratic regulations.
>
> (Karasimeonov, 2008, p. 5)

Apart from the tendency already outlined of understanding populism as a movement, this definition provides several other key elements – the presence of discontent in a specific social-economic and political situation, anti-elitist attitudes, aspiration to a radical change of the status quo, but the fact that its political manifestation, apart from radical or anti-systemic can also be systemic within the framework of democratic rules. This is a significant moment as regards the process of populism gaining dominance and its spread among the so-called systemic parties, including such as may have to prove their identity through affiliations with European party families, and also during the time they are in power.

So far, one can summarise that populism can coexist with other ideologies; that it is not a display of non-democratism, and – as seen from the Bulgarian case – it emerges in a moment when democracy in the country is actually being solidified and that it arises in a vacuum (most frequently ideological) and as a result of discontent, and that despite of its anti-systemic character it can function as a part of the system, that is, power. As we shall see later, however, "systemic" populism can turn out superseded by "anti-systemic".

Certain account of the appearance of populism on the Bulgarian scene is provided by Anna Krasteva in a survey analysis of the phenomenon in its Bulgarian context. It analyses the factors, conducive to the emergence and advance of post-communist populism at two levels – external and internal.

External factors include the absence of the Cold War and the globalisation. The first is associated with the readjustment of political priorities:

> The end of the Cold War has rearranged the order of political priorities. During the Cold-War period, there was corruption, too, but this issue was not so much at the center of public opinion; today it is one of the top five issues in Bulgaria as well as in many other countries.
>
> (Krasteva, 2013)

Globalisation, as reminded by Krasteva, occurs for Bulgarians simultaneously with Europeanisation: "During the first decade of the transition both were perceived positively, as an alternative to closed communist society. Paradoxically, it was precisely when European integration from a project became a fact that Euroscepticism began to intensify" (idem).

Krasteva divides the internal factors into social, ideological, and political. To Krasteva, social factors comprise the social basis of political identifications and attitudes towards politics (Krasteva, 2013). There are four circles around which these are construed: first, the increasing sense of the transition as being unjust, as neglecting people in favour of swindlers; in the second place, the crisis of representativeness; in the third, the extremely low confidence of Bulgarian citizens in the Parliament and the political parties, and the extremely widespread opinion that elections cannot bring about fundamental change ("frustration of democracy", as in Smilov, 2008); in the fourth place, the absence of working, open, and responsible institutions (Krasteva, 2013). Along with the ideological factors, Krasteva outlines the oppositions traditional for the early post-1989 years, convergence of the policies, which unsettles traditional distinctions along the left-right axis and the increasingly crucial role played by symbolic policy, which employs forceful mobilising resources such as (anti)Europeanism and nationalism (Krasteva, 2013). The political factors relate to the exhaustion of the already mentioned oppositions, the decline of reformist right-wing parties and the crisis, mostly ideological, of the socialist party (Krasteva, 2013). Other authors define the trend in terms of "electoral vacuum" (Zhdrebev, 2019), wherein "actors with light ideological and organizational baggage can find their place" (Smilov, 2008, p. 26). It is precisely in this vacuum that populist projects originate, such as the movement around Simeon Saxe Coburg-Gotha (NMSS) and subsequently around Boyko Borisov (GERB), and on a next stage, as we shall see from the 2021 wave, a range of new formations.

Another point of interest in Krasteva's analysis is the attempt to assign classification to various populist parties and movements. She introduces the terms soft and hard populism. Here are some proposed definitions: "Soft populism involves general appeals to the people, catch-all politics and demagogic discourses. The main representatives are the former King Simeon and Prime Minister Boyko Borisov (2009–2013)" and "Hard populism is nationalist, extremist, and xenophobic, with an emphasis on Othering. At the moment, its active restructuring is in progress" (Krasteva, 2013). Between the two outlined formats, she positions the IMRO, and most likely the reason to do so is found in the statement:

> The party's discourse varies from more moderate to more aggressive, depending on the political conjuncture, its coalition partners, the competition in the nationalist niche, the fluctuations in political identification; the discourse tends towards either the pole of nationalism or the pole of contestation.
>
> (Krasteva, 2013)

As of 2013, this classification already has its arguments and validity. What is of interest to our analysis is the intermediate form. In the first place, in a purely formal sense, because of the subsequent role of the IMRO in the political life of the country and particularly with regard to migration. And in the second place, due to the possibility for soft and hard formats and of other actors to converge in this "intermediacy" in a way that would render the entire political spectrum "infected" with populism. In our understanding, the convergence between mainstream and radical/far-right or extremist parties does not lead to the taming of the latter, but rather to the shifting of the entire spectrum of the political system and in the first place, to undermining the process of producing effective policies by replacing them with *politics of fear* (Wodak, 2020).

As we have seen, "classic" populist parties in the country, mostly from the patriotic and extremist spectrum, have been for a long time of marginal significance to the political life and received comparatively peripheral electoral support, but coalitions from the entire political range have been a steady presence in the National Assembly, as we have shown. Krasteva has synthesised this as a paradox: "National populism emerged on the Bulgarian political scene in the form of a democratic paradox. In the 1990s, democracy was fragile, but there were no extremist parties; once democracy was consolidated, extremist parties appeared and achieved success" (Krasteva, 2016, p. 164). By and by, however, they came into their own in terms of ideas and actual parliamentary presence.

Undoubtedly, the analysis of Kiril Avramov is the closest to our understanding (Avramov, 2015, p. 299). Avramov proposes the terms 'generic' and radical right instead of soft and hard populism. Tracing in detail the changes in the political system after 2001 based on this differentiation he outlines the tendency of mainstreaming in its incipience:

> However, the general impact of the process of mainstreaming Ataka was GERB's adoption of some of the most abrasive standards, resulting in a growth of hate speech and intolerance in public life. The lack of a cordon sanitaire and the porosity between the mainstream and the margins has shifted the entire system to the right, and the tactics of "taming" the "marginals" actually produced a radicalization of the mainstream instead. Additionally, new issues are coming up in the Bulgarian context that appear to provide a real "stress test" for the immune system of the relatively young, transforming Bulgarian democracy. Such challenges include the institutional challenge of coping with pressure [of migrants coming] from Asia and Africa, and sanctioning aggressive and abrasive behavior by populist radical right leaders, even if they are represented at parliamentary level, as was the case with Siderov. Dealing with the revival of Islamophobia will be another such test.
>
> (Avramov, 2015, p. 315)

The cooperation between GERB and Ataka has opened wide the doors in subsequent years precisely for this process of mainstreaming, which has ultimately led to a complete shift of the centre of the political system and to the transformation of populism into a dominant factor. At a later stage, Avramov's statement has transpired in the coalitional politics of GERB dominated by the logic of the "indispensable (sine qua non) government". This practice has served on the one hand, to legitimise smaller and more extreme parties such as Ataka, IMRO and NFSB by their direct inclusion into the government as a junior government partner. On the other hand, to ensure some form of stability to government, in practice government has come closer to the spectrum of the extreme in a range of areas and public sectors[2]:

> ... strategy was to integrate right-wing populists with the aim of neutralizing them through government responsibility and, hence, disenchanting them by disclosing their incapacity for power. However, this strategy also turned out to be ineffective in recent constellations of neoliberal austerity policies and growing global mobilities. Instead of taming right-wing parties through integration we are witnessing a mainstreaming of right-wing populism. For instance, the National Front for Salvation of Bulgaria (NFSB)[3] since 2014 has been the smallest partner in the three-party governing coalition in Bulgaria but dominates the formulation and implementation of numerous policies, especially migration and refugee policies.
>
> (Pajnik and Sauer, 2018, p. 21)

In practice, this has "introduced an 'opportunistic' form of politics for 'buying' the support of the voters rather than looking at 'best options' in policy solutions (Mudde, 2004, p. 542)" (Pajnik and Sauer, 2018, p. 22) and at the same time

> populism as a "discourse" (Mudde and Kaltwasser, 2012a., p. 3) succeeded in introducing new discursive settings and agendas by neglecting the complexity and long-term consequences of political decisions through creating a "highly emotional and simplistic discourse that is directed at the 'gut feelings' of the people" (Mudde, 2004, p. 542).
>
> (Pajnik and Sauer, 2018, p. 22)

If the advent of the first big populist projects – NMSS and GERB, and in 2005 – of national-populism with the Ataka, movement – have made it possible to speak of emptied space in the right side in relation with the first, "democratic" projects of the transition period, understood as the systemic political actors; but also, for example, such as the establishment of market economy – with the second, the emptying of ideological substance of the parties of the left spectrum (the party – BSP) has served in recent years as a catalyst, which in the poorest European member state has opened fertile space for the emergence of anti-systemic (mostly leftist) projects or ones that are rather liberal in terms of values (culture), which on the other hand are far from the expectations of the traditionally left electorate in economic or social respect (Table 4.1). This does not mean that there is in evidence a left populism in Bulgaria (certainly not in the reading of Chantal Mouffe (Mouffe, 2018), simply the space freed from a genuinely left-wing party was occupied mostly by populism. This tendency has acquired particular visibility at the 2021 elections. Following the mass protests from the summer of 2020 which heightened the demands for change of the corrupt government in which business and state were connected,[4] several projects of purely anti-systemic, populist character have emerged ("Rise up! Oust the Thugs!" (ISMV), civil platform "Bulgarian Summer",[5] "There are Such People" (There is Such a People/Nation or This is the People)). Although the protests failed to overthrow

Table 4.1

Prime Minister	Beginning of Office	End of Office	Coalitional Partners
Saxe Coburg-Gotha	24 July 2001	17 August 2005	NDSV, MRF, The New Time
Stanishev	17 August 2005	27 July 2009	BSP, NDSV, MRF
Borisov 1	27 July 2009	13 March 2013	GERB (The government does not have majority in Parliament and was elected with the support of Ataka, the Blue Coalition and the party of Order, Legality and Justice).
Raykov	13 March 2013	29 May 2013	provisional; independent
Oresharski	29 May 2013	6 August 2014	BSP, MRF (The government does not have majority in Parliament and was elected with the support of Ataka).
Bliznashki	6 August 2014	7 November 2014	provisional; independent
Borisov 2	7 November 2014	27 January 2017	GERB, Reformatory Bloc, ABV
Gerdazhikov	27 January 2017	4 May 2017	provisional; independent
Borisov 3	4 May 2017	-	GERB, United Patriots

Source: Authors

the government and to lead to early elections, the great surprise at the regulars was the second place won by There are Such People, from which they displaced BSP. There are Such People was founded by one of the famous television presenters in Bulgaria, showman and crooner Stansilav Trifonov,[6] and it is not a coincidence that it is named after one of his most popular music albums. The party originated when Trifonov and his scriptwriters promoted the idea of a referendum, which was conducted in 2006.[7]

Not just the name of the party emphasises the "people", Trifonov's discourse fits distinctively into Margaret Conavan's conception according to which the people is imagined as a "mythic being that is not only the source of political legitimacy, but can sometimes appear to redeem politics from oppression, corruption, and banality" (Canovan, 2005, p. 123). Taguieff stresses that people can be considered as demos or as an ethnos. On this basis one can define two main types of anti-elitist interpretations. In the case when the people are regarded as "demos" we are referring to common people, sharing common values, wisdom, ethic, and spirit of sacrifice. In this type of understanding, we have a vertical antagonism, which Taguieff calls 'protestatory populism', which sees the elite as discreditable to represent the citizens. When the people are regarded as 'ethnos', they are attached to the national idea; and Taguieff describes this as 'identitarian populism' (Taguieff, 2002, p. 123). In the case of There are Such People and Trifonov, however, we have grounds to believe that "protestatory populism" and "identitarian populism" converge.

The breakdown of the votes from abroad is interesting. There was a record high overseas electoral activity.[8] In the first ten parties which garnered more substantial electoral support one can detect mainly populist elements. Outside the country, the victor is the new populist entity There are Such People, with GERB – which is first in the national vote – ranking only fourth with a modest 8.66% of the votes. Substantial support was received also by formations such as Vazrazhdane and Bulgarian National Alliance, for which we said in another occasion that they fall precisely within the populist spectrum. Substantial support was also received by the "protest" parties such as "Rise up! Oust the Thugs!" as well as "Democratic Bulgaria", whose success could be accounted for with a protest vote and with the line of contraposition of the elite (in this case governmental) and the people (in the case of the formations as embodiment of popular discontent and the alternative) (Table 4.2).

The great paradox, however, is that an extensive analysis again indicates that the political system is completely shifted to the right and the conservative (respectively, in terms of economy and values) and

Table 4.2 Summarised data from the overseas vote for the election of National Assembly representatives (top 10)

Party, Coalition	Votes	Distribution of Votes
Political Party There are Such People	52,317	30.75%
Democratic Bulgaria – an alliance (Yes, Bulgaria! Democrats for Strong Bulgaria The Green Movement)	29,889	17.57%
Movement for Rights and Freedoms	23,004	13.52%
GERB-UDF	14,725	8.66%
Vazrazhdane ("Revival")	12,647	7.43%
BSP For Bulgaria	11,098	6.52%
Bulgarian National Alliance*	9,011	5.30%
Rise up! Oust the Thugs!	7,241	4.26%
Political Party IMRO – Bulgarian National Movement	2,673	1.57%
Patriotic Coalition – Will and NFSB	907	0.53%

Source: Authors after data from the National Institute of Statistics

Table 4.3

Populists of the Transition	New Populists
GERB	There are Such People
BSP	Rise up! Oust the Thugs!
United Patriots	Bulgarian National Alliance*
	Vazrazhdane ('Revival')

Source: Authors

that although the great clash is between the status quo and the change (Dinev, 2021).

In practice, we are witnessing how new digital populist projects[9] displace the populist, analogous projects of the transition after the apt definition of Strahil Deliyski (Deliyski, 2021) (Table 4.3).

It should be noted that although IMRO, Ataka, and NFSB remained outside the Parliament, there are 10% of voters, who are ready to vote precisely for such a type of "bravado patriotism" (Pamporov, 2021). Also, part of their vote flows to Trifonov and There are Such People. In this case there can be no question of their disappearance from the political stage and – as noted by Moffitt, even if they disappear, they may have "significant long-term cultural and institutional effects" (Moffitt, 2020, p. 9).

The 2021 elections have brought migration back to the agenda in an interesting way. The political crisis of the populists is solved by creating another crisis. A short time after the regular elections and in the eve of upcoming irregular elections,[10] the resigned Prime Minister, and a leader of GERB launched an intensive fake news campaign. In it, along with the subjects of the corruption and violations, the topic of migration was once again introduced. One of the things, in which the government was taking pride, in addition to the construction if highways, was the good control if the "illegal" migration. It is precisely along this line, after a long, almost zero presence during the electoral campaign and the months of pandemic, the topic of the "migration problem" was brought back. In several consecutive media appearances, Borisov reminded of it in "formidable" nuances:

> Just for the past 3 days we have prevented 323 attempted ingresses of illegal migrants into Bulgaria. I am saying this for my opponents, because as of today we have allowed zero illegal migration. This was accomplished with the immense effort if our celebrated border troops, for which I am grateful to them. The pressure is formidable, they invade form all sides – from Greece and from Turkey.
>
> (BNR, 2021)

It seems that in the context if the coming elections and in view of the enormous outflow of voters, the aim is to remind that the "unwanted migrants" are controlled successfully only because of the effort of GERB and mainly in the person of Boyko Borisov. In the years this suggestion has been made several times, but the most vivid example is that of the beginning of the Covid-19 pandemic, when a telephone conversation between President Erdogan of Turkey and Prime Minister Borisov rerouted thousands of migrants towards Turkey's border with Greece rather than with Bulgaria. The topic was immediately taken up also by the resigned military minister and IMRO leader:

> The border pressure from emigrants from Turkey is a question of political decisions on the part of Turkey. Turkey has always been using emigrants to exert pressure on Europe. (...) The question is whether we are willing to accept certain naive and inane European propositions, or we shall stand for the position precisely if non-admission if illegal immigrants on the territory of Bulgaria (...) I emphatically continue to believe that Bulgaria should not participate in negotiations of any kind and should not give any consent for some quotas which in Europe shall be redistributed to other European states.
>
> (Stephanov, 2021)

Our hypothesis is that once brought back, the topic shall be actively exploited by all political parties.

This is the point to remark that a huge role in the transformation of populism into a norm was played by the media. The media, and television in particular, are responsible for producing quite a lot populist leaders in Europe. Bulgaria is no exception in this sense. Ataka rose to prominence on the political scene not without the help of television. Slavi Trifonov, for his own part, has been on screen from the early 1990s. What is characteristic about the Bulgarian case is that in the context of strongly dependent media environment[11] through intensifying if extreme discourses and providing a platform, journalism, instead of serving as resource and platform to combat these phenomena and act as a protector of democratic values, proved the main accomplice in the process of normalisation of populism. Moreover, the media "has contributed to the mainstreaming of the populism in three main ways: agenda-setting power and deflection, euphemisation and trivialisation, and amplification" (Brown, 2020). One should keep in mind as well that normalisation if populism is happening through processes on many levels: "Normalization processes encompass the incorporation if fringe ideologies into the mainstream – not only if politics but if popular culture and other fields as well – through re-contextualization and re-semiotization procedures" (Wodak, 2020, p. 59).

Based on this survey of the literature by Bulgarian authors, which has also allowed us to introduce chronologically the development of populism in Bulgaria, which led to the point of its becoming a norm, a dominant in the political process of the state, we could delineate several key moments. The first is related to the formation of the party system, the exhaustion of the transition cleavages and the transformation of party politics into symbolic politics. The second relates to the way in which the market economy was built in the country, with the merging of economy and state, the disintegration of the social systems, and the distances of the citizens from the institutions and the political overall. The third is related to the role of the media and the digital turn.

In the following lines we shall attempt to answer the question, what kind of crisis it is that we observe, as we use migration as a turnsole to outline the tendencies.

Crisis of?

"Populist insurgency" is a term which has found broad usage mostly in the media in order to describe the turning against the established elites, institutions, and parties, and the intensification of the nationalistic moods around the so-called "migration crisis" – the culmination of a process which had begun a little earlier in the aftermath of the Arab Spring of 2011 (Campani, 2019, p. 29). Campani again, however, reminds that this is not a crisis of numbers: "it is a question of 'narratives' that has to be understood in the framework of a global and European process of political, economic, social and cultural transformation" (Campani, 2019, p. 29). This fact has validity in the Bulgarian context. As we have seen in the previous chapters, although the number of asylum seekers and mixed migration flows has grown abruptly, only to fall later within quite normal and non-crisis borders, it is precisely the narrative of migration that generates the crisis. This narrative is a product both of politicians and other "power holders" such as media and intellectuals (Inglehart and Norris, 2016 in Campani 2019. In the commercial struggle for audience, media discourse tends to privilege sensationalism, often presenting migration as a threat, and simplistic visions of "Us vs. Them", including essentialising uses of the notion of culture (Dervin, 2013). This is notably the case in the context of "deep mediatization", characterised among other things by the fragmentation of media audiences and the associated polarisation of politicised discourse (Couldry and Andreas, 2016; Hepp et al., 2018).

The case of Bulgaria is of particular interest as regards the process of mainstreaming in the context of the "migration" crisis. Campani (Campani, 2019) rightly differentiates the attitude taken by the left-wing and the right-wing to migration:

> The refusal to accept new incoming flows of migrants – even if they are escaping from conflicts – and the rejection of multicultural society is one of the topics in which "right-wing populism" or " national-populism" (Taguieff, 2002) and "left-oriented populism" differ. In the case of populism, the cultural cleavage appears to be more important than the economic ideas. Right-wing populism tends in fact to unify "the people" (...). Progressive groups such as Syriza and Podemos tend, on the contrary, to show solidarity towards migrants and refugees, as being generally the weakest components of the society. (...) The same "progressive populism" may, however, be very critical of the impact of the migration processes on the economies both of the global North and the global South.
>
> (Campani, 2019, p. 31)

As we have seen repeatedly in this text, in Bulgaria there is no left-wing populism in this sense. BSP, a traditionally left-wing party, introduced the innovative leftist conservatism with which it entered the competition for the most extremist attitude towards migration together with the far-right and nationalist formations and the rest of the mainstream actors, while a new breed of populism originates in the space emptied of authentic progressive leftism, which however, is also more of the patriotic kind. Campani herself sees the reasons for the disintegration of the left, understood as social-democratic, in its embracing of "neo-liberal values, placing the market at the core of the economy, subordinating politics to it, had heavy consequences on the social fabric" (Campani, 2019, p. 36). In this manner,

> The sense of being politically abandoned has been most acute within sections of the traditional working class, whose feelings of isolation have increased as social-democratic parties have cut their links with their old constituencies. As mainstream parties have discarded both their ideological attachments and their long-established constituencies, so the public has become increasingly disengaged from the political process. The gap between voters and the elite has widened, fostering disenchantment with the very idea of politics (Kenan, 2017).
>
> (Campani, 2019, p. 36)

Ruth Wodak reminds in this sense that in the states of Central and Eastern Europe the historical context is different. Superimposed on the one hand are collective memories either of fascist regimes, or of complicity to such,[12] and on the other – of the communist past: "at least two histories have to be integrated into collective memories: on the one hand World War II, and on the other, the communist era and various forms of resistance" (Wodak, 2020, p. 258). In addition to this past, which often engenders contradictory narratives in the collective memory, the transition to democracy and mostly to market economy has established new categories of winners and losers:

> Many wanted to become part of "the West" as quickly as possible, others wanted to remain neutral, and yet other groups nostalgically longed for "the better past" (...). The very different memories and experiences in Western Europe and Eastern Europe serve, at least, as a partial explanation for different political developments and different kinds of far – right populist movements and their programs, for different electorates and gender politics, and for the different scapegoats: Muslims and so – called "illegal migrants"

in Western Europe, Muslims, Jews, homosexuals and Roma in Eastern Europe.

(Wodak, 2020, p. 259)

Bulgaria has verified very emphatically this claim. As already noted, when talking of Bulgaria, one should bear in mind that the disillusionment stems not only from the loss of connection between traditional parties and their electorate, but also from the way in which the process of democratisation and of establishment of market economy – the so-called transition – has taken place, as well as from the fusion of government and business, from the extremely high corruption levels,[13] the non-transparent process of decision making and the dysfunctional social systems and institutions. In addition, as shown earlier in this text, the "visible" migrant appears much later, but in a very appropriate moment. It is precisely in a situation where normalisation of populism has already commenced that politics of fear has found its rightful place (Wodak, 2015, 2020). This complex process was aptly summarised as a process of transition from "class politics to value politics, from party politics to symbolic politics, from ideological to identity politics, from socio-economic to cultural cleavages" (Krasteva, 2016).

To see, however, how fear is being built, we need to see first how the whole, which is to be defended, is constituted.

It seems that if there is certain agreement in relation to populism, it is that populism is constructed along the "people – elite" dichotomy. Canovan synthesises this as "an appeal to the people against established structures of rules, power as well as against the society's dominant ideas and values" (Canovan, 1999, p. 2). The phrase suggested by John B. Judis and Ruy Teixeira is even shorter: "the people versus the powerful" (quoted in Mudde, 2004, p. 543). Among Bulgarian researchers Smilov talks about a form of ideology which opposes the people to the elite (Smilov, 2008), while Malinov emphasises that populism is always against the elites, be they economic, political, cultural (Malinov, 2008). Anti-elitism as an element of populism is widely studied. Panizza (Panizza, 2005, p. 141), for example, states that "populism is a [discourse] against the status quo, [simplifying] the political space, by symbolically dividing society between the people and others". On his part, Cas Mudde (Mudde, 2004, p. 161) defines populism as an 'ideology with a thin center which [holds] that society must finally be divided into two homogeneous and antagonistic groups, "pure people" versus "corrupt elites" and in this sense politics must be the expression of a general will of the people.

In the Bulgarian context, this contraposition, as well as its populist instrumentalisation, has also found support in the civic culture which has been gaining in popularity in the recent years. The contestatory citizen feels less and less represented by the systemic parties, has increasingly lower trust in the classic institutions whereas at the same time is highly digitalised and reactionary. In this connection it is to be reminded that the new channels of civil spirit and civil commitment are not infrequently radical and contestatory (Taguieff, 2002). In this sense, anti-elitism is a natural response and a reaction of the citizens which defy the status quo, the politicians, the elites – national and supranational. The traditional parties become less and less successful on fulfilling the expectations of these citizens. Therefore, it is not by accident that there are new actors springing up on the political scene ready to transform the civil energy, to channel the radical moods and frequently, fears as well.

This accounts to a great extent the high electoral result both new formations, represented by There are Such People, and of those parties which in the Bulgarian context are being called "parties of the protest". On the other hand, it is possible that precisely the rapprochement between the parties from the nationalistic spectrum with the elite is one of the reasons for their poor electoral performance.[14]

Jan-Werner Müller emphasises that postwar logic in Europe and the process of European integration limit to a certain degree the will of the people by way of supranational limitations. This essentially anti-totalitarian and anti-populist logic, however, makes of Europe an especially vulnerable target for political actors speaking on behalf of the people against a system which limits its participation (Müller, 2016, pp. 52–53). These new forms of representativeness, originating with the European integration, which often tend to be extremely indirect, widen the distance between the elites and the citizens (Taggart, 2002, p. 75). Müller at the same time evaluates in a similar manner the role of the current crises and although in his opinion nit every crisis might entail a populist wave, the problem in EU is the way in which it responds to problems – technocracy. "Technocracy holds that there is only one correct policy solution; populism claims that there is only one authentic will of the people" (Müller, 2016, p. 97). Populism often simplifies the political space, by symbolically dividing society between the people and others (Panizza, 2005, p. 141). Community carries exceptional weight in the populist notion of the people inasmuch it is constituted solely by its authentic representatives (Meny and Surel, 2002, p. 12). Yves Mény and Yves Surel write that populism rejects the horizontal cleavages – for example, along the line left-right, but also introduces vertical ones through which it excludes the elites and the foreigners. The other one may have different faces: the cultural other – a representative if ethnic or religious minority, of sexual minority, the migrant; the political other – the elite, certain ideologies such as multiculturalism; the supranational other – the European Union, international organisations such as the World Bank, the International Monetary Fund, or even foreign investors and organisations supposedly financially supported by external donors.

Often the talk against these others is superimposed with negative representations mutually reinforcing each other (Jehel et al., 2015). On this occasion, Kamenova and Pingaud write:

> The "other-migrant" is becoming one of the favorite subjects in the discursive logic of the confrontation between difference and sameness typical of right-wing populism. (...) This newly found enemy, the migrant, plays so [vividly] the role of the "other" that it often replaces more typical subjects such as traditional minorities. In Bulgaria, for instance, if once nationalistic and xenophobic arguments were the Turkish and Roma minorities as well as European institutions that treat Bulgaria as a "second category member state" (Styczyńska, 2015, p. 205), today's immigration is [being increasingly] exploited by right-wing populist actors.
>
> (Kamenova, 2018, p. 111)

Here is, for example, a quotation of a representative if IMRO in the European Parliament, which wonderfully demonstrates the superimposition of the discourses against the others:

> ...There here to make a war. (...) Do not forget to render thanks for this invasion to the obnoxious hypocrites, the double-faced pseudo-liberals. Do not fail to remember the Helsinki Committee, the Friend of the Refugees, the whole grant-receiving scum. (...) What they deserve is to gather them together, together with that sociologist woman, the minister in resignation, and shove them into this camp, so that their pet darlings, their cherished wards could "enjoy" them in accordance with their tribal traditions and cultural peculiarities. (...) This swinishness, this outrage can no longer be tolerated. (...) This is our land, our native country and we shall protect it.
>
> (Epicenter, 2016)

It is precisely this superimposition of many forms of "otherness" that transforms the migrant into the most convenient "other" for the political forces in Bulgaria, which successfully "instrumentalize and evoke a range of moral emotions, such as anxiety, fear, resentment, anger, rage, shame and nostalgia" (Wodak, 2020, p. 46), reaching different levels of society. With some this takes place through securitarian logics, with others – through the deduction of primordialist and ethnic arguments, with third through welfare nationalism. In many cases the argumentation is overlapping and it is difficult to use it as an indicator of the political identity of certain actors which is characteristic of populism and populist parties.

Politics materialises in (lack of) policies. The other, the different, is being excluded either through an iron fence (the reception policies), through non-admission to the national body (the suspended integration policies): "the 'postmodern strangers' are to be kept outside" (Wodak, 2020, p. 255) in every sense. An extremely illustrative example of how politics kill policies is the attempt to follow an established European practice within the logic of absorbing European funds and appealing to our partners, with the integration of status recipients brought to a local level. The Decree 208 of August 2016 on the adoption of Ordinance on the Conditions and Procedures for Conclusion, Enforcement and Termination provides for an agreement on the integration of foreign nationals who have been granted asylum or international protection. Apparently, the document attempts to implement decentralisation in the realm of refugee integration, making provisions for the active involvement of local authorities. The Ordinance rules that Bulgaria should fulfil commitments undertaken before the EU and envisions that local municipalities should obtain funding to carry out integration of refugees by providing them with housing, children schooling, kindergartens, and work. According to voices from within the nationalist parties, rather than regulating the integration of foreign nationals who have already acquired a refugee status, the focus of the document were illegal immigrants: "There is a semi-secret decree of the Council of Ministers concerning illegal immigrants. The issue at hand is that some municipalities shall be enabled to accommodate illegal migrants" (Frognews, 10.10.2016). The emergent "front" against the resolution which, besides the nationalists, also included representatives of other parties, such as the Bulgarian Socialist Party (BSP). The leader of the left-wing BSP sees in it a threat to the social rights of Bulgarian citizens:

It is too much that Bulgarians will have to contend for equal rights with refugee families which will be accommodated in the country, and mayors are compelled to provide them with housing, to pay their health insurances and to support them for the issuing of Bulgarian documents.

(Pan, 2016)

"and opines that the idea to solve demographic problems by accommodating refugees is the ultimate cynicism" (Cross, 2016) and calls for an end to the "servility to European institutions and Merkel" (Btv, 2016).

There was not a single municipality to participate in the programme, and the decree was repealed by the interim government, appointed by the incoming President, nomination of BSP, although the same government had adopted a text featuring no substantial alterations of the previous document. The succeeding regular government of the GERB party adopted still another version of the text, which again lacked any essential changes. The ordinances were elaborated within intradepartmental panels which did not comprise all concerned actors or and failed to include diverse partners.

At the end of the previous section of the present chapter we made a point of using migration as a kind of turnsole to help us outline some tendencies. It is not a coincidence that it is called "A crisis of..." The normalisation of populism in Bulgaria became most visible through the topic of migration, which has made an abrupt entry on the agenda – political and societal – after the country found itself located on the Balkan Refugee Route. The tendency, however, comes because of a much deeper crisis. We were in position to trace various populist waves, which led to its gradual transformation into a norm. The last wave allowed to the greatest extent to observe how populism evoked more populism. Bulgarian society is highly polarised, institutions are being perceived as "vacuous" and a crisis of trust is in evidence. In this environment, symbolic policies and the policies of fear have found an extremely beneficial ground. One of the greatest problems, however, is that these conditions have created a closed circle, where in less and less real policies and solutions are being offered, which on its part generates more and more distrust.

In this sense, the greatest crisis is the crisis of trust. Politics in the area of migration is a very good example since they are extremely easily transformed into affective and display the entire process of impossibility for policies to be made.

Notes

1 After 2001
2 A number of examples can be given, some of them already mentioned in the preceding chapters – migration is one of them, but we can add the rejection of the Istanbul Convention, the suspended changes in the Law for Protection of the Child, the position on Macedonia's membership in EU.

3 The quotation mentions NFSB, but IMRO and "Ataka", who are part of the coalition, play the same role.

4 In addition to the resignation of the government, the protests also demanded the resignation of the attorney general (chief prosecutor).

5 The party was founded in 2020 by Vasil Bozhkov, considered to be the wealthiest Bulgarian with assets estimated at between 1 and 3 billion leva. In January 2020 Bozhkov left the country and escaped in Dubai to avoid detention after a number of charges were brought up against him, including those related to murder, money laundering, tax evasion, rape, etc. On the 2021 parliamentary election the civil platform "Bulgarian Summer" ran under the mandate of another party, Bulgarian National Alliance (BNO) and won 2.95 of the electoral votes.

6 Stanislav "Slavi" Trifonov began his career on the 1990s at the student television programme "Coo-Coo", and later was a producer of its successor, the programme "Canaletto" which assumed a leading role in the protests against the Zhan Videnov government (BSP, 1995–1997). From 2000 to 2019 is the anchorman of the "Slavi's Show". Through his producer's house he released a number of other television productions. As a musician, together with the Coo-Coo Band headed by himself, he released a number of music albums, concerts, and tours across the country (thus, for example, they were particularly actively involved in the campaign for the release of the Bulgarian medical nurses, detained in Lybia by the Gadaffi regime on charges of intentional spreading of AIDS infection). In 2019 started the Seven Eights TV (Seven Eight (7/8) is an unequal music meter popular in Bulgarian folk music and used in Trifonov's music). Actually, the part initially tempted under the name "There is No Such State", but the Supreme Courts of Cassations denied entry permission due to established violations of the Law of Political Parties.

7 The enterprise committee headed by Trifonov and the script writers of his television programme proposed the following questions: (1) Are you in favour of the members of parliament being elected via majoritarian electoral system with absolute majority on two rounds? (2) Are you in favour of the number of members of parliament being reduced to 120? (3). Are you in favour of the introduction of mandatory voting on elections and referenda? (4). Are you in favour of remote voting and electronic voting being allowed in the course of elections and referenda? (5). Are you in favour of fixing the annual government subsidy for financing the political parties at one leva for one actual vote received at the last parliamentary elections? (6). Are you in favour of the directors of the regional directorates of the Ministry of the Internal Affairs and the heads of the regional administrations at the regional directorates of the Ministry of the Internal Affairs being voted through majority electoral system with absolute majority in two rounds?

   After these were widely discussed in his program, the Initiative committee submitted in the Administration of the National Assembly a total of 673,481 signatures for the enacting of referendum. The institutions established 572,650 valid data, nearly 200,000 more than required by law. In the following months, the National Assembly voted another set of changes in the Election Code, President Plevneliev approached the Constitutional Court on some of the questions. Eventually, the referendum was held together with the presidential elections in November 2016 with three questions: (1). Are you in favor of the members of parliament being elected via majoritarian electoral system with absolute majority on two rounds? (2). Are youn favor of mandatory voting being introduced on elections and referenda? (3). Are you in favor of the annual government subsidy granted as a financial support to the political parties and coalitions being fixed at one leva for one actual vote received at the last parliamentary elections?

In the end, the activity on the vote failed to reach the levels required for the vote to carry binding force. In the following years the referendum and the results are intensely / forcefully instrumentalised by various political actors.

8 Over 170,000 Bulgarians abroad have voted on the Parliamentary elections in 2021. In comparison – at the last parliamentary elections, less than 120,000 Bulgarians have voted from abroad.
9 IDN are exceptionally active on the Internet, where their television is also already streamed.
10 The attempts to form a government were unsuccessful.
11 Bulgaria is the state with the most problematic media climate in EU for 2020. This is indicated by the Index for Press Freedom for 2020 of Reporters without Borders, which covers 180 states. In this index, Bulgaria occupies 111-th position. The country is on the last place in freedom of speech in ES.
12 Bulgaria participated in WWII on the side of the Axis and the government of the country is (pro)fascist, although this has become subject of discussions after 1989.
13 The annual Index of Corruption Perception for 2020 of the international anti-corruption organisation "Transparency International" indicates that Bulgaria continues to be among the countries with the highest "corruption perception" in the European Union (EU), but as opposed to past years, when it was found alone at the bottom in the Community, in 2020 it has shared this place with Romania and Hungary.
14 Another reason for their low results is found in their decision to run on the elections not as coalition, but as individual formations.

Bibliography

Avramov, K., 2015. The Bulgarian radical right. Marching up from the margins. In: M. Minkenberg, ed. *Transforming the Transformation? The East European Radical Right in the Political Process.* London: Routledge, pp. 299–318.
BNR, 2021. *Bulgarian National Radio.* [Online] Available at: https://bnr.bg/post/101462757/borisov-predupredi-za-migrantski-natisk-po-granicite-ni [Accessed 5 May 2021].
Brown, K. M., 2020. Populism, the media, and the mainstreaming of the far right: The Guardian's coverage of populism as a case study. [Online] Available at: https://doi.org/10.1177/0263395720955036.
Btv, 2016. *Btv.* [Online] Available at: http://btvnovinite.bg/article/bulgaria/politika/kornelija-ninova-vidja-sluginazhpred- es-i-merkel-za-bezhancite.html [Accessed 10 May 2021].

Campani, G., 2019. The migration crisis between populism and post-democracy. In: G. Fitzi, J. Mackert and Bryan S. Turner, ed. *Populism and the Crisis of Democracy Volume 3: Migration, Gender and Religion*. London: Routledge, pp. 29–47.

Canovan, M., 1981. *Populism*. New York: Harcourt, Brace, Jovanovich.

Canovan, M., 1999. Trust the people! Populism and the two face of democracy. *Political Studies*, 47(1), pp. 2–16.

Canovan, M., 2002. Taking politics to the people: Populism as the ideology of democracy. In: Y. Mény and Y. Surel, ed. *Democracies and the Populist Challenge*. New York: Palgrave, pp. 25–44.

Canovan, M., 2005. *The People*. Cambridge: Polity Press, p. 123.

Cholakov, P., 2017. Populistkata radikalna desnitsa v Bulgaria: predstaviteli, proizhod, ideologia, horizonti. *Politicheski Izsledvania*, 75–89.

Couldry, N. and Andreas, H., 2016. *The Mediated Construction of Reality*. Cambridge: Polity Press.

Cross, 2016. *Cross.bg*. [Online] Available at: http://www.cross.bg/ninova-obshtinite-bulgariya-1521112.html#.WISprFN97cs [Accessed 10 May 2021].

de la Torre, C., 2018. *Populisms. A Quick Immersions*. Kindle Edition: Tibidabo Publishing.

Dinev, I. D., 2021. [Online] Available at: https://www.dnevnik.bg/izbori_2021/2021/04/12/4197042_politicheski_kompas_na_izborniia_rezultat/?fbclid=IwAR0igKtFL3zjmIqeGw918jR_Uh-joYJg95PHc92Z-OVCAolkFQje9avc3Mw

Epicenter, 2016. *Epicenter*. [Online] Available at: http://epicenter.bg/article/Angel-Dzhambazki--Buntat-v-lagera-v-Harmanlitryabva-bade-smazan-Te-sa-tuk-za-voyna-/114835/2/0 [Accessed 10 May 2021].

Frelick, B., Kysel, I. M. and Podkul, J., 2016. The impact of externalization of migration controls on the rights of asylum seekers and other migrants. *Journal on Migration and Human Security*, 4(4), pp. 190–220. [Online] Available at: http://jmhs.cmsny.org/index.php/jmhs/article/view/68.

Gattinara, P. C., 2020. *Populism, Radicalism and Extremism: At the Margins and into the Mainstream*. [Online] Available at: https://ecpr.eu/Events/Event/SectionDetails/911 [Accessed 6 April 2021].

Hepp, A., Breiter, A. and Hasebrink, U., 2018. *Communicative Figurations: Transforming Communications in Times of Deep Mediatization*. Basingstoke: Springer Nature.

Inglehart, F. R. and Norris, P., 2016. Trump, brexit and the rise of populism: Economic have-nots and cultural backlash. Faculty Research Working Paper Series, Harvard: Harvard Kennedy School.

Jansen, R. S., 2011. Populist mobilization: A new theoretical approach to populism. *Sociological Theory*, 29(2), pp. 75–96.

Jehel, S., Kamenova, D. and Otova, I., 2015. Conclusion. In: M. Ranieri, ed. *e-Engagement against Violence: Tools for Media and Citizenship Education*. Rome: ARACNE International, pp. 195–201.

Kamenova, D. P., 2018. Anti-migration and Islamophobia: Web populism and targeting the "easiest other". In: M. S. Pajnik, ed. *Populism and the Web*

Communicative Practices of Parties and Movements in Europe. London: Rutledge, pp. 108–121.

Karasimeonov, G., 2008. Ima li poniatieto populisum nauchna stoinost. *Politicheski izsledvania*, Issue 1.

Kenan, M., 2017. Populism and migration. Pandemonium. [Online] Available at: https://kenanmalik.wordpress.com/2017/10/05/populism-and-immigration/.

Krastev, I., 2007. Populistkia moment [Populist moment]. *Eurozine*.

Krasteva, A., 2013. *Bulgarian populism*. [Online] Available at: https://annakrasteva.wordpress.com/2013/12/25/bulgarian-populism/

Krasteva, A., 2016. The post-communist rise of national populism: Bulgarian paradoxes. In: G. Lazaridis, G. Campani, and A. Benveniste, eds. *The Rise of the Far Right in Europe Populist Shifts and 'Othering'*. London: Palgrave Macmillan, pp. 161–200.

Malinov, S., 2008. *Radical demophilia Reflections on Bulgarian populism*. [Online] Available at: Eurozine: https://www.eurozine.com/radical-demophilia/

Medarov, G., 2017. Istoricheski kontekst i politicheski zalozi na diskursivnata teoria na pipulisma. *Politicheski izsledvania*, 1–2, pp. 56–74.

Meny, Y. and Surel, Y., (eds), 2002. *Democracies and the Populist Challenge*. s.l.: Palgrave.

Moffitt, B., 2020. *Populism*. Cambridge: Polity Press.

Morley, J. and Taylor, C., 2012. Us and them: How immigrants are constructed in British and Italian newspapers. In: P. Bayley and G. Williams, ed. *European Identity: What the Media Say*. Oxford: Oxford University Press, pp. 190–223.

Mouffe, C., 2018. *For a Left Populism*. London: Verso.

Mudde, C., 2004. The populist Zeitgeist. *Government and Opposition*, 39(4), pp. 541–563.

Mudde, C., 2007. *Populist Radical Right Parties in Europe*. Cambridge: Cambridge University Press.

Mudde, C., 2016. *On Extremism and Democracy in Europe*. London: Routledge.

Mudde, C. and Kaltwasser, C. R., 2012a. Populism and (liberal) democracy: A framework for analysis. In: C. Mudde and C. R. Kaltwasser, ed. *Populism in Europe and the Americas: Threat or Corrective for Democracy?*. Cambridge: Cambridge University Press, pp. 1–26.

Mudde, C. and Kaltwasser, C. R. 2012b. Populism: Corrective and threat to democracy. In: C. Mudde and C. R. Kaltwasser, ed. *Populism in Europe and the Americas: Threat or Corrective for Democracy?*. Cambridge: Cambridge University Press, pp. 205–222.

Mudde, C. and Kaltwasser, C. R., 2013. Populism. In: M. Freeden and M. Stears, ed. *The Oxford Handbook of Political Ideologies*. Oxford: Oxford University Press, pp. 493–512.

Müller, J. W., 2016. *What Is populism?* Pennsylvania: University of Pennsylvania Press.

Pajnik, M. and Sauer, B. (eds), 2018. *Populism and the Web: Communicative Practices of Parties and Movements in Europe*. Abingdon and New York: Routledge.

Pamporov, A., 2021. [Online] Available at: https://www.dnevnik.bg/
izbori_2021/2021/04/07/4195464_piianstvoto_na_edin_elektorat/
?fbclid=IwAR0Ph1NDZFtqoiCJwSb4vaq4ccJcJfRqG409ls4gpKkp
ED846wq4SLri3t4).

Pan, 2016. *Pan.* [Online] Available at: http://www.pan.bg/view_article-
61-356500-Korneliya-Ninova-Bylgarite-tryabvada-se-boryat-za-ravni-prava-
s-bezhanci-i-s.html#sthash.zn6Itkrr.dpuf [Accessed 10 May 2021].

Panizza, F., 2005. *Populism and the Mirror of Democracy.* London: Verso.

Pappas, T., 2019. What makes Popilists and Nativists Distinkt. In: s.l.:s.n.

Rheindorf, M. and Wodak, R., 2019. "Austria First" revisited: A diachronic
cross-sectional aanalysis of the gender and body politics of the extreme
right'. *Patterns of Prejudice*, 53(3), pp. 302–320.

Smilov, D., 2008. Bulgaria. In: D. Smilov, G. Meseznikov, and O. Gyarfasova,
eds. *Populist Politics and Liberal Democracy in Central and Eastern Europe.*
Bratislava: INSTITUTE FOR PUBLIC AFFAIRS, pp. 13–36.

Smilova, R., 2020. *Theoretical Model of Causes of Populism.* s.l.: s.n.

Sommerbauer, J.,2007. Ataka Bulgaria: Every Path Leeds to Nationalism.
Café Babel. [Online]

Stephanov, V., 2021. *Dir.bg.* [Online] Available at: https://dnes.dir.bg/
politika/vazmozhna-li-e-patriotichna-koalitsiya-za-11-yuli-otgovorat-
na-krasimir-karakachanov [Accessed 6 May 2021].

Styczyńska, N., 2015. (Non)existence of Bulgarian party-based euroscepticism
– Why should we care? Politeja. *Journal of Faculty of International and
Political Studies*, 33, pp. 201–214.

Taggart, P., 2002. Populism and the pathology of representative politics. In:
Y. Meny and Y. Surel, ed. *Democracies and the Populist Challenge.* s.l.:
Palgrave, pp. 62–80.

Taguieff, P. A., 1995. Political science confronts populism: From a conceptual
mirage to a real problem. *Telos*, 103, pp. 9–43.

Taguieff, P. A., 1997.Le populisme et la science politique: Du mirage
conceptual aux vrais problèmes. *Vingtième siècle*, 56, pp. 4–33.

Taguieff, P. A., 2001. *The Force of Prejudice: On Racism and its Doubles.*
Minnesota: University of Minnesota Press.

Taguieff, P. A., 2002. *L'illusion populiste: De l'archaïque au médiatique.* Paris:
Berg International.

Taguieff, P. A., 2004. *Le retour du populisme: Un défi pour les démocraties
européennes.* Paris: Universalis.

Taguieff, P. A., 2007. *L'illusion populiste: Essai sur les démagogies de l'âge
démocratique.* Paris: Flammarion.

Taguieff, P. A., 2012. *Le nouveau national-populisme.* Paris: CNRS.

Todorov, A., 2016. The extreme right wing in Bulgaria. In: M. Mlinaric, S.
Goll, and J. Gold, eds. *Minorities under Attack Othering and Right-Wing
Extremism in Southeast European Societies.* Göttingen: Otto Harrassowitz
GmbH & Co. KG, Wiesbaden, pp. 277–294.

Wodak, R., 2015. *The Politics of Fear What Right-Wing Populist Discourses MeanSA*. London: SAGE.

Wodak, R., 2020. *The Politics of Fear the Shameless Normalization of Far-Right Discourse*. Kindle Edition: SAGE.

Zhdrebev, A., 2019. *Populizmut kato faktor za disfunktsia na politicheskite institutsii v Bulgaria (2001–2018)*. Sofia2: Iztok-Zapad.

5   When policies are absent, is solidarity present?

This chapter is devoted to solidarity which comes in response to dominant populism. We will do this via several entries on the topics. On the one hand, we are going to analyse solidarity as a possible and compensatory mechanism of coping with the crisis. Solidarity shall be examined via the institutionalised forms (national and international), as well as via non-formal civil networks and organised civic structures. With that we shall discover how they replace the missing policies of the state.

The connection between increasing migratory flows and the crisis of solidarity is axiomatic. In fact, the increase in the number of applications for international protection always generates a debate on solidarity, whether on global, European, or national level (Wagner et al., 2018, p. 5). Moreover, observations already made available indicate that solidarity and cooperation seem to be moving backward and not forward (Krunke and Petersen, 2020, pp. 1–8). The refugee crisis in Europe is indisputably one of the examples, but the subsequent Covid crisis has also inflicted serious damages with regard to solidarity, especially on transnational level. It will hardly be an overstatement to say that not just on a national level but also on European level solidarity is in crisis.

In a national aspect this was particularly conspicuous on an institutional level – providing adequate measures for protection and meeting even of the existential necessities of seekers and recipients of asylum in the country in the country which was transformed in missing integration policies or in erecting a fence, many notifications made by human-right organisations for incidents of push-back on the border or the declared instances of violence or derogation of human rights of migrants amount to glaring examples not just of non-functional institutions, of absence of policies, due to the domination of populist

DOI: 10.4324/9781003161493-6

politics, but also of the utter absence of solidarity with those in need of support on an institutional level. On European level, the solidarity debate focusses mainly on sharing the "burden" and the expenditures proceeding from the reception of foreigners between EU member states. In this sense on a community level, solidarity is more often understood as such between individual national states and more rarely in terms of solidarity with migrants themselves. While the European elites were debating about the approach in solidarity and the countries from the Visegrád Four took emphatic stand for their positions, this debate was almost absent in Bulgaria.

It should be noted that paradoxically the combination of migration pressure and the flourish of populism have also evoked manifestations of solidarity. Against the backdrop of the national and to a certain degree European collapse thus described the representative bodies of several international organisations to Bulgaria have made efforts through expertise, direct humanitarian aid, information campaigns, etc., to help alleviate the severity of the crisis. Outside the ground of the institutions on a national level, despite the serious levels of social distances and stable symbolic universes of rejection, there emerged some remarkable examples of civil involvement and support, which indicate that individual citizens, grassroots initiatives, and organisations can succeed in mobilising actively in support of vulnerable groups and, in particular, of migrants.

The first section of the text is dedicated to the role of the international organisations and the EU. In the second we shall explore solidarity in the context of civil activity.

External assistance: the role of international organisations and the EU

We have already pointed out on another occasion, that Bulgaria has recognised migration as an issue of political order only at an extremely late stage, but in view of the transition to democracy and the endeavour to harmonise legislation with international standards, as early as the beginning of the 90s it began to construct a system for reception of international protection seekers. In this sense, it is hardly surprising that in July 1993 the UN High Commissariat for Refugees and the Government of the Republic of Bulgaria entered an official agreement, which effectively started the mandate of UNHCR in the country. In 2008, together with Romania, Bulgaria joined the UNHCR Regional Office for Central Europe, which also includes the Czech Republic, Hungary,

Poland, Romania, Slovakia, and Slovenia. The role of UNHCR in Bulgaria is to assist, consult, and to intercede in partnership with the governments and the non-government organisations to ensure:

- effective access of asylum seekers to the territory of EU and asylum-granting procedures.
- continuous monitoring and improvement of living conditions for asylum seekers in reception centres and other refugee facilities, as well as guarantees regarding their age, sex, and specific needs.
- equitable and effective procedures of granting a refugee status in compliance with international legal standards.
- finding of permanent solutions through effective integration and resettlement policies, as well as encouraging a more positive social climate and attitude to refugees, as well repudiation of xenophobic and racist moods (UNHCR, 2016).

It should be noted that in the years UNHCR Bulgaria has realised a range of projects, among them research and analyses important to the understanding of the refugee issue in Bulgaria, as well as several social projects and initiatives with other organisations specifically addressing the improvement of the situation of asylum seekers and the recipients of status. In recent years, such have been the labour-exchanges organised by UNCHR, where employers from all over the country have an opportunity to meet representatives of the refugee community in the country who are actively looking for jobs. One of the most recent initiatives, organised by UNCHR in cooperation with the Refugee Advisory Council,[1] is a platform to combat rumours about refugees.[2] The platform is intended to provide reliable and relevant information on refugee problems both to the Bulgarian society and the refugee communities. Thanks to the active work of these organisations, as well as the co-optation of several national partners, including civil society organisations and volunteers, the increase in the flow of asylum seekers and migrants making a transit passage through the country did not reach the proportions of a severe humanitarian crisis.

Bulgaria is also an IOM member since 1994, with a Cooperation Agreement between Bulgaria and IOM officially entering into force 2000. Ratified by the National Assembly and followed by a Decree of the President of the Republic of Bulgaria, it provides the IOM Mission in Bulgaria the same privileges and immunities as those of UN Specialized Agencies under the Convention on the Privileges and Immunities of the Specialized Agencies of 1947 (IOM Bulgaria). The two organisations have lent substantial assistance to the State of

Bulgaria in the years. Their role proved extremely important after the abrupt increase in the number of migrants in the years after the country found itself located on the Balkan Refugee Route. As we have already seen, the response of the state can be considered a failure in many respects. Basic needs of asylum seekers were not met; the conditions on the reception centres were beyond any admissible international standards. Flourishing populism, soaring xenophobia, fear of terrorism, and demonisation of refugees and migrants contributed to the creation of a chaotic situation wherein the state has abdicated from its duties. Bulgarian legislation does not explicitly provide for or guarantee access to reception centres for international organisations. In practice, they are allowed the freedom to operate in the reception centres once they sign a partnership agreement. The partnership agreements are signed on individual basis with the respective NGO or any other international organisation, usually on the initiative of the international or the non-governmental sector. Their role is of extraordinary significance to the system's functioning. Currently, the Mission of IOM Bulgaria consists of a head office in Sofia and a regional Migrant Information Centre for legally residing migrants in Burgas. Another field office operates at Harmanly. According to the organisation's own declaration:

> IOM Bulgaria seeks to assist the government in the development and implementation of migration policies that respond effectively to modern migration realities and challenges, aiming at the optimal balance between observing the principles of free movement of people, controlling irregular migration and protecting the human rights of migrants. IOM strives to help build stable migration management structures responsive to the increasing external migration flows, stimulate regular and prevent irregular migration, diversify the services offered to migrants and inform the public on all issues and aspects of migration. Given the public and social importance of trafficking in human beings, IOM Bulgaria will continue to follow its long-term strategy, assisting the development of national mechanisms to combat and counteract trafficking in human beings and support victims of trafficking.
>
> (IOM Bulgaria)

The second essential element, which gives an impulse and exerts influence on the development of migration policy in Bulgaria after the 90s, is the process of accession and the actual membership in the EU. Here, to a very great extent one can speak mostly of the harmonisation of the national and European legislation to ensure implementation of criteria subject to factors not directly connected with the awareness or specific comprehension of migration. This tendency began within the framework of the pre-accession process and continues into the following years, including after the beginning of the crisis. Practically, as a member of CEAS, Bulgaria has transposed the EU directives in the area. The evaluation of the experts is that the trend is rather a positive one, although occasionally it is used in EU law for the enactment of restrictions.

From what has been described so far, it becomes clear that the state strives to comply with the standards of international and European law at least as far as documents are concerned, or – as we have said on another occasion in the previous chapters – the Europeanisation of migration policy, as well as many other things, may happen "on paper" but to a much lesser extent in practice.

Often, the European Union is perceived as nothing more than a donor of financial resources. The following chart, displaying data from the European Commission, reveals the amount of financial resources invested by separate European funds in the area of migration in Bulgaria.

Interestingly, despite the large financial amounts, as of the onset of the crisis in 2012 the system was found completely even in material aspect unprepared.

If we examine the unfortunate Ordinance on the conditions and order of conclusion, implementation, and termination of integration agreements with foreigners with granted asylum and international protection, we shall see that among the cited sources of financial support. It is the European funds that are cited in the top, such as Asylum, Migration and Integration Fund, operational programmes under the European Social Fund and the European Regional Development Fund, and the Fund for European Assistance to the Most Deprived. These are followed by international and foreign financial instruments such as the Norwegian Financial Mechanism, etc.; resources from international institutions and organisations, whereas the possibility for national financing is mentioned only in the last place (Bulgarian Council on Refugees and Migrants – BCRM). Experts in the field are most often critical of the state for its lack of information on the expending of the resources, as well as of the measures, for which they are most often utilised: "Fragmentary and sparse publicly available information indicates that there are European funds available, but their allocation is primarily for border protection, governance of migration flows and repatriation of illegally residing migrants" (Vankova et al., 2017).

In view of what has been said so far, it is hardly a surprise that, paradoxically, although Bulgaria has practically harmonised its asylum legislation with that of the European Union, one can hardly speak of Europeanisation of the migration topic, but rather about its nationalisation and closure in the local debate. Missing, for example, is a substantive discussion on quota redistribution or a national debate on the revision of the Common European Asylum System. "The long summer of migration can be qualified as mainly a crisis of refugee reception in Europe or even a crisis of European solidarity because of the lack of agreement on how to distribute the task of handling the migration", as Andrea Rea, Marco Martiniello, Alessandro Mazzola, and Bart Meuleman write in the introduction to *The Refugee Reception Crisis in Europe Polarized Opinions and Mobilizations* (Rea et al., 2019). Bulgaria was not among the bright stars in this debate.

An interesting study based on media monitoring over the period May–November 2015 (that is, the period of active discussions on quota distribution) and the parliamentary debate give a fair idea as to how the debate in European solidarity translates into Bulgarian context. The huge body of articles is purely informative, with the largest number of publications associated with the period of most intensive traffic on the Balkan Refugee Route, and not so much with the period of debating of the specific EU propositions of quota distribution and later, the schemes of relocation. As of 2015, there are still to be found distinctly varying viewpoints. The one of the pro-European and liberal camps has a very vivid exponent in the person of President Plevneliev. We remind that he initiated together with the Prime Minister Oresharski a declaration condemning attacks on migrants and social displays of hatred (see Chapter 4). There is an interesting observation that in the government incumbent at the moment – Borisov 2 – different voices are heard (Krasteva et al., 2018). Thus rulers end up as the platform of divergence of the discussions on the topic. As we have seen in Chapter 2, it was in this period that the Parliamentary season opened with declarations on migration – made byte BSP and the Patriotic Front. The GERB rulers maintained symbolic silence. Anna Krasteva resumed the debate in three points.

> Firstly, the refugee policy was politicized through the mobilization of the opposition. Both BSP and the patriotic coalition were opposition parties in the 43nd Bulgarian Parliament. Secondly, there was no polarization, because the predominant securitization of the refugee policy came from opposite ends of the political stage: more timid and moderate in BSP's case (at least for the time

being; later on, BSP would embrace nationalist rhetoric more enthusiastically); extreme, uncompromising and fierce in the nationalist interpretation. Thirdly, de-responsibilization from the EU policies for governance of the refugee crisis.

(Krasteva et al., 2018)

This example is a clear verification of the thesis that at a European level there is no debate on solidarity and the conversation is closed within the parameters of the national political process. We have seen how politicisation of the migration topic has subsequently unfolded. The debate on European solidarity EU has found a new impulse with the New Pact on Migration and Asylum proposed in 2020. To many, the key element in the "principle of solidarity" is the understanding that it is mostly a matter of will, since in the opposite case it would be more an obligation than "solidarity". It should be noted that the new Pact has made a proposition which comes closer to the understanding of "solidarity by understanding". In practice, this formulation can bring European politics nearer to normativity than to solidarity as a principal factor of European integration, related to the concept of European legitimacy (Raspotnik et al., 2012). As expected, no talk about the pact took place in Bulgaria.

This is the place to note that the formalisation of the role of EU especially as regards migration governance, also including the absence of a national debate on the essence of the suggested mechanisms and programmes, is again related to dominant populism. Populist anti-elitist discourses and moods which we have commented upon in the previous chapter of the book are often with a reference to Euroscepticism. The European elite is being accused not just for not coping convincingly with the crisis, but also for not representing the interests of the citizens but, on the contrary, makes decisions in their detriment. The need of transfer of sovereignty towards supranational institutions has been increasingly questioned by populists. In this sense the European suggestions of solidarity, for instance, in the distribution of asylum seekers, have been viewed as endangering the national security and as an infiltration channel for foreign influence, foreign population and together with it – foreign culture.

As we have seen so far, the role of the international organisations and EU is of essential importance to the development of Bulgaria's migration policies. Very often this is a key role to the stabilisation of the reception system in the context of a crisis, to give one example. Unfortunately, the process is very often reduced to formal harmonisation of legislation and development of policies and measures solely with the purpose of fund absorption. In the years of the so-called "refugee crisis" Bulgaria has completely verified the assertion that what is dealt with here is mostly a solidarity crisis – institutional and national. In the context of normalisation of extreme and populist discourses and practices, and of politicisation of the migration topic, the debate on solidarity on European level does not take place in practice, but in the contrary, is being nationalised and confined within the dynamics of the national political process.

Friends of the refugees: NGOs and civic activism

Solidarity has found its place in a situation of dominant anti-migrant sentiment through NGOs and informal networks. Social networks, the wave of civic mobilisations and new forms of civil spirit have created vivid images of solidary citizens supporting asylum seekers. Equally interesting is the role of the migrants of older standing (veteran migrants) which, although but a few, are well integrated.

Óscar García Agustín и Martin Bak Jørgensen suggest three types of solidarity: autonomous solidarity, civic solidarity, and institutional solidarity (Agustín and Jørgensen, 2019, p. 39). They have suggested the following definition of "civic solidarity":

> Civic solidarity indicates ways of organizing produced as civil society initiatives to include refugees. It counts a vast number of manifestations and actors, such as NGOs, local communities, and individuals. It is practiced by civil society that is not part of the state, but the degree of contention varies depending on the claims and strategies of each organization.
>
> (Agustín and Jørgensen, 2019, p. 41)

Solidarity movements in Bulgaria can be examined in parallel with similar movements from across the world and analysed in the context of global tendencies. The specific situation of their origin, however, and the specificities of the environment wherein they originate should also be understood. In Central and Eastern Europe, the downfall of indigenous communist regimes gave rise to certain expectations that civil society would emerge as the main factor in the process of democratisation. It is seen as a "sine qua non condition for democracy" (Todorov, 2009), as a "training ground that 'grooms' citizens, preparing them for civic participation and political engagement" (Dahlgren, 2006, p. 272). Anna Krasteva writes that the non-governmental organisations are the "translation" of the post-communist civil society

(Krasteva, 2009, p. 37). Paradoxically, however, it turns out that, in order to promote civil society, it is structures and not activities, organisations and not citizens that receive greater support (Krasteva, 2012).This has brought about certain distortions of the civic sector, which can be brought down to two negative trends – institutionalisation and professionalisation (Otova, 2013). Radosveta Krestanova explains that: "the modus operandi of the non-governmental organizations as an organizational culture 'imported' into Bulgarian environment often acquires a corporative character, which can make them seem closer to business organizations and impedes citizens in recognizing them as organizations operating for the public benefit" (Krastanova, 2012, pp. 14–15).

This period in the development of the civic sector, coinciding with the process of democratic transition in Bulgarian society, is governed by two clearly defined purposes: the building of consolidated democracy and market economy (Otova, 2013). The results, however, were far from positive: distortions invaded both the civic sector and the political process, and an irresponsible business-environment was allowed to take shape. Tsvetan Todorov summarises this transition in terms of values as the passage from communist mirage to capitalist wilderness (Todorov, 2017, p. 32). In this sense, the democratic deficit, the discredited institutions, the apparent lack of ethics and morality – both in the political and the market domain – can also serve as a key drive and catalyst in the acts of Bulgaria's civil activism.

If the first period was marked by the domination of the NGO, the next was dominated by the advent of a new generation which was itself a product of the transition – one that was raised and formed in the process of democratisation, bearing the marks both of its pluses and biases (Otova, 2013). As it happened, the digital turn took place simultaneously with these developments. Or, it is in the context of this increasingly digitised world that the concept of citizenship acquired a special significance. A relatively novel topic for the Bulgarian research field, it was introduced and asserted by Anna Krasteva. Citizenship pertains not just to a legal status, but is also loaded with engagement, action and activity. "Technology becomes socially condensed and acquires sense only by becoming implicated in political transformation", writes Anna Kristeva, who believes that the 'digital citizen' is the political project of Internet (Krasteva, 2013). He/She will eventually emerge as the key actor, who strives to revitalise the democratic process, rationalising it through the new digital prism.

One of the most innovative studies on the subject is that of Anna Krasteva "Being a Citizen in Times of Mainstreaming of Populism:

Building Post-communist Contestatory and Solidary Citizenship" (Krasteva et al., 2019). In this "program" text, post-communist civic agency is conceptualised through the theoretical perspectives of Donatella della Porta's diffusion model (Della Porta, 2015), the acts of citizenship (Isin and Nielsen, 2008), and A. Kristeva's contestatory citizenship (Krasteva et al., 2019, p. 214). The choice is for theorising civic resistance and responses to post-communist far-right populism through the conceptual lenses of citizenship are substantiated by four reasons: "During communism, citizenship was understood as status and belonging, as integration into the state; one of the democratic innovations of post-communism was citizenship as 'consciously assumed responsibility'" (Carter, 2001, p. 10), as participation, activism, and contestation. The second reason is the development of the concept as a heuristic tool for understanding and explaining the diversification of civic mobilisations. Anna Krasteva has elaborated the concepts of e-citizenship, green, contestatory, and creative citizenship (Krasteva et a.l, 2019); this article aims to elaborate solidary citizenship. The third reason is that citizenship expresses the transition from NGOs to "acts of citizenship" (Isin and Nielsen, 2008) from the engineered project of building a civil society to the emergence of new forms of civic agency. Post-communism has been criticised for its lacking political imagination; its beginning has been conceptualised as an end: "the end of history" (Fukuyama, 2006). "Citizenship remains a significant site through which to develop a critique of the pessimism about political possibilities" (Isin and Nyers, 2014, p. 9). It is precisely the active and positive potential of citizenship in generating change and change-bearers that served as our fourth reason for selecting this concept for the analysis of post-communist activism (Krasteva et al., 2019, pp. 214–215).

Krasteva has outlined three groups of post-communist citizenship, by indicating for each of them the relevant mobilisation type and adversary:

- eco, environmental – Business lobbies – Green
- occupy, mass protests – Oligarchization/State capture – Contestatory
- humanitarian, Anti-racism, Human rights – Mainstreaming of populist securitization – Solidary (Krasteva et al., 2019, pp. 210–235).

In the following passages we shall use the following typology for the examples we are about to adduce: non-governmental organisations; non-formal groups and volunteers, supported or not by the social media; solidarity of the migrant communities.

Although the formal structures of the non-governmental sector, as we have said, are characteristic of the post-1989 years, they have played a no small role in assisting the work of the institution in the area of migration in the years of the so-called migrant crisis. Very often, without support from them, migrants and protection seekers would be left with no support altogether. In this sense, one can see in the non-governmental organisations working in the area of migration, certain reversion to the authentic role of the civil sector, void of "professionalization" and a focus on find absorption. Non-formal groups and the volunteers fit entirely into Kristeva's conception of solidarity citizenship. We have marked off the solidarity for migrant communities into a separate group inasmuch as they are, on the one hand, the connecting link in the migration history of Bulgaria. On the other hand, their quite more essential role of active citizens, embodied in solidarity citizenship, is an example of "empowerment" of the migrant through his/her own engagement in society. Their support for newly arrived migrants is not viewed within the narrative of the classic migration theory of networks, but in the sense of acts of citizenship "acts of citizenship" (Isin and Nielsen, 2008).

Non-governmental organisations are the key actor everywhere in Europe: "Civil society organizations were often the first to provide language and educational support for refugee children" (Crul, February 2017, p. 2).

There are two large international organisations working actively in Bulgaria. The first is the Bulgarian Red Cross, and in particular – the agency for refugees and migrants, established in 1997. The organisation is one of the principal actors with respect to social integration and orientation of migrants in Bulgaria. This role was confirmed at the time of the migration pressure of 2015, when the institutional collapse and the ensuing lack of integration programmes were filled with a wide spectrum of activities of the BRC and other partner organisations. These which can be highlighted include:

- support of foreigners which are found in a status-granting procedure including social consultations, accompanying and translation on visits to government and municipal institutions, medical institutions, as well as support for the education of the children educated in Bulgarian primary and secondary schools.
- assisting the social and economic integration of foreigners to whom the State Agency of Refugees has granted refugee status or humanitarian status. This direction includes activities from conducting Bulgarian language courses for persons who have

received international protection through assisting the access to medical help and services; assistance in finding jobs; social and cultural orientation.

• assistance to foreigners who have expressly wished to seek protection in Bulgaria and subsequently detained in the border sectors, as well as to foreigners who have been accommodated on special facilities for temporary accommodation of foreigners, through providing humanitarian aid – food, clothing, medication, etc.

In addition to working directly with the refugees, the Bulgarian Local Service of the Bulgarian Red Cross works to fortify the civil society of Bulgaria by contributing to the formation and institutional development of non-governmental refugee organisations. In addition, with the help of media partners and information campaigns, the Bulgarian Red Cross strives to overcome the stereotypes about refugees by engendering towards them an attitude of acceptance and tolerance.

Another international organisation which is in solidarity with the problems of the refugees and migrants, is Caritas. For individuals who have acquired refugee or humanitarian status, the St. Anne Centre with Caritas Sofia operates in the capital, providing social consultations, psychological support, Bulgarian Language Courses, assistance for finding jobs, art occupations, mentorship programme, and other activities supporting the process of integration into Bulgarian Society. For people seeking asylum, accommodated in the reception centres with the State Agency of Refugees, Caritas Sofia organises activities with occupational and recreational character for children, youths, and women, Bulgarian language courses, science, art and sport as well as preparation courses in Bulgarian language for children in pre-school age. For individuals inhabiting the Busmantsi and Lubick provisional accommodation centres, Caritas Sofia organises informal educational activities and art occupations (Caritas). For asylum seekers accommodated at the reception centres of the State Agency for Refugees, Caritas Sofia implements: "Refugees project", through which volunteers participate in activities for training and education of children, young people and elderly people such as lessons in Bulgarian and English, cooking courses, applied arts, music, theatre and other kinds of activities. Caritas implements also "Play and Learn" project, through which Caritas employees organise play and entertainment activities for children and youth, Bulgarian language lessons, science, arts, sports, as well as preparatory courses in Bulgarian for children of school age. One can hardly be exhaustive in presenting the entire list of non-governmental organisations working in the area,[3] the main fields of activity provided by them include: legal assistance, support in finding jobs; psychological support.

An example of informal group is Refugees and Friends of the Refugees. This informal group of volunteers won the big prize "The Human of the Year" of the Bulgarian Helsinki Committee for 2013. Friends of the refugees emerged as a Facebook group and along with donation actions and campaigns, it has engaged in particular cases – from acquiring prams for babies to finding a doctor fluent in Arabic, or from responding to request to find rented lodgings to advertisements of employers, willing to hire immigrants. In the initial months of the crisis, volunteers contrived to appropriate the function of a defaulting state and to provide assistance to asylum seekers – from food all the way to clothing and sanitary materials. Numerous campaigns, most of them organised in social networks, have filled the defaulting measures.

At the beginning of the analysis, it was mentioned that the immigration picture in Bulgaria is atypical – the few well-integrated immigrants remain unnoticed by society. Most of them are well integrated by the labour-market, owners of small and medium business ventures. Similar is the characteristic of the Syrian community in Bulgaria. With the crisis in full swing, the assistance they extended to the new arrivals had a life-saving effect. We will represent it in two illustrations.

He is the owner of one of the fast-food franchises in Bulgaria. In the first months of the crisis, he undertook to ensure victuals to new arrivals through continuous donations. Over the years, he has provided employment to many asylum seekers and individuals who were granted status and has continued supplying humanitarian aid to the SAR Centres.

She is one of the most active members of the Syrian community in Bulgaria and a volunteer who was always on the forefront from the initial phase of the crisis. In the following years, she never ceased working in assistance of refugee centres with various campaigns and non-governmental organisations, expanding its activities also to centres in Greece.

One of the most active organisations at the time of the crisis had been founded several decades precisely by refugees. The Council of Refugee Women in Bulgaria, since its establishment in 2003 until today, has been actively working on site and in cooperation with almost all representative bodies of international organisations on the county. In 2004 started the provision of humanitarian aid and support – one of the services maintained by the association until today. The main factor in building the programme for humanitarian aid is related to the understanding of the donors, their responsiveness and empathy.

Over time, corporate donations, which constitute a major portion of our humanitarian programme at the moment, are gaining increasing popularity and significance. The programme places a special priority on the entry of individuals looking for protection, unaccompanied minors, as well as individuals in a grave social, medical and economic condition – divided mothers and fathers, widowed spouses, people who have lost their relatives and have remained in their own, families with many children, aged individuals, and children with severe medical and psychological traumas.

Another major area on the association's agenda is the social mediation. Through the social mediation programme, people seeking protection receive opportunities for direct access to social assistance in the form of translation and facilitation of communication, accompanied visits to government institutions, social consultation and information, coverage of emergency health and social expenditures for vulnerable people. The same support is made available by the Union of the Women Refugees in Bulgaria to people who have received international protection and who have settled to live in Bulgaria. They receive assistance in their effort to adapt to a different and unfamiliar social, medical, and educational system. Social mediators provide assistance on cases related to the education – enrolling into schools and kindergartens, social information and access to social services in the community (The Council of Refugee Women in Bulgaria).

Another inspiring example comes not from other refugees or migrants from the Middle East, but from two English women, a mother, and a daughter, who started as volunteers to become inspirers, establishing from scratch a school for refugees on one of the camps in Bulgaria. In 2015, there were 300 days passing through their classroom daily, between 4 and 14 years of age, whom they taught English but mostly provided an opportunity for them to have fun and top forget the war they were running from (Drumeva, 2015).

Solidarity is a major force in transforming a society and in challenging migration and asylum policies from below (Agustín and Jørgensen, 2019). It often arises in situations of contestation, as opposition to systems of domination and exclusion (ibid). When the government policy follows the logics of closure and exclusion in the national territory or national body through restriction of access or missing integration policies, the practices of solidarity with the migrants and refugees can be understood as an assault on the established political order (Bauder, 2020). In the context of normalisation of populism, these acts of contraposition of the leading discourse of politicians, media and other actors of broadly conceived power may have a particularly important meaning. In the Bulgarian case already with the first documents in the area of migration, which rely heavily on ethnocentric and primordia list logics we have seen that solidarity is understood within the border of the ethnic nation. This tendency has intensified in the process of politicising of migration in the years after the outset of the so-called refugee crisis, in which the dominating narratives perceive the migrant, the postmodern foreigner, either as an outsider, swallowing the nation, or culturally other (far-right, nationalists), or as a competitor for the social foods (in a greater extent, the left). In this sense, the examples of solidarity with the migrants are of exceptional importance. The role of the non-government organisations, which replace missing policies, is of key importance to their survival. But the informal networks are those who take a real stand against the leading narrative, by proposing a different reading to the society. The activity of the migrants from the older communities should in no case be viewed in terms having ethnic character or, as already stated, to be understood in the context of the network theory – it is a demonstration of real acts of citizenship which not just offer support to those in need, but aim to change dominant attitudes, narratives and logics of power to achieve a transformation of society.

Notes

1 Refugee Advisory Council (RAC) is also a UNHCR recent project that aims to help refugees assume a leading role in the making of policies, which directly influence the integration and welfare of these communities with an emphasis on the integration on city level. The Council shall function with the support and under the supervision of UNCHR Bulgaria.
2 https://rumorfree.org/
3 Quite a full list of them is, for example, prepared by the Center for Studying Democracy   https://csd.bg/bg/publications/publication/directory-of-institutions-and-organizations-working-with-selected-vulnerable-groups/

Bibliography

Agustín, Ó. and Jørgensen, M., 2019. *Solidarity and the 'Refugee Crisis' in Europe.* s.l.: Springer International Publishing.
Bauder, H., 2020, December. Migrant solidarities and the politics of place. *Progress in Human Geography*, 55(6), pp. 1066–1080.
BCRM, n.d. *Bulgarian Council on Refugees and Migrants.* [Online] Available at: https://www.refugee-integration.bg/източници-на-финансиране/ [Accessed 21 March 2021].
Caritas, n.d. *Caritas Bulgaria.* [Online] Available at: https://caritas.bg/en/causes/refugees/activities-refugees/ [Accessed 5 April 2021].

Carter, A., 2001. *The Political Theory of Global Citizenship*. 1 ed. London: Routledge.

Crul, M., February 2017. Refugee children in education in Europe. How to prevent a lost generation? *SIRIUS Network Policy Brief Series*, Issue 7. Available at: https://www.sirius-migrationeducation.org/wp-content/uploads/2018/10/Refugee-children-in-education-in-Europe.-How-to-prevent-a-lost-generation.pdf

Dahlgren, P., 2006. Doing citizenship: The cultural origin of civic agency in the public sphere. *European Journal of Cultural Studies*, 9, pp. 267–286.

Della Porta, D., 2015. *Social Movements in Times of Austerity: Bringing Capitalism Back into Protest Analysis*. s.l.: John Wiley & Sons.

Drumeva, E., 2015. *Time Heroes*. [Online] Available at: https://blog.timeheroes.org/post/121908174662/klasna-staya-bezhanski-lager-harmanli [Accessed 5 April 2021].

Fukuyama, F., 2006. *The End of History and the Last Man*. March 1, 2006 ed. s.l.: Free Press.

IOM Bulgaria, n.d. *IOM Mission in Bulgaria*. [Online] Available at: https://www.iom.bg [Accessed 20 March 2021].

Isin, Engin F. and Nielsen, Greg M. (eds), 2008. *Acts of Citizenship*. London and New York: Zed Books.

Isin, Engin F. and Nyers, Peter (eds.), 2014. *Routledge Handbook of Global Citizenship Studies*. Routledge International Handbooks ed. London: Routledge.

Krastanova, R., 2012. *Green Movement and Green Parties in Bulgaria: Between System Integration and System Change*. Sofia: Friedrich Ebert Foundation.

Krasteva, A., 2009. Being a citizen – Not a profession, but a commitment. In: K. Hristova-Valcheva, ed. *New Actors in a New Environment: Accession to the EU, Civil Society and Multi-level Governance*. Sofia: BECSA.

Krasteva, A., 2012. *Du citoyen postcommuniste au citoyen connecté*. [Online] Available at: http://anna krasteva.wordpress.com/2012/02/10/du-citoyen-postcommuniste-au-citoyen-connecte/ [Accessed 6 April 2021].

Krasteva, A., 2013. Grazhdanski protesti, e-demokratsia, novi mobilizatsii [Civil protests, E-democracy, New Mobilizations]. In: A. Todorv, and D. Kanev, ed. *Kachestvoto na demokratsiyata v Balgaria [The Quality of Democracy in Bulgaria]*. Sofia: Iztok-Zapad.

Krasteva, A., et al., 2019. Being a citizen in times of mainstreaming of populism: Building post-communist contestatory and solidary citizenship. In: A. Krasteva, B. Siim and A. Saarinen, ed. *Citizens' Activism and Solidarity Movements*. Cham: Palgrave Macmillan, Palgrave Studies in European Political Sociology, pp. 213–241.

Krasteva, A., Siim, B. and Saarinen, A., (eds), 2018. *Citizens' Activism and Solidarity Movements. Contending with Populism*. s.l.: Palgrave Macmillan.

Krunke, H. and Petersen, H., 2020. Introduction. In: H. Krunke, H. Petersen and I. Manners, ed. *Transnational Solidarity: Concept, Challenges and Opportunities*. Cambridge: Cambridge University Press, pp. 1–8.

Otova, I., 2013. Ekologichnite mobilizatsii v Balgaria [The ecological mobilizations in Bulgaria]. In: A. Krasteva, ed. *Digitalniyat grazhdanin [The Digital Citizen].* Sofia: NBU, pp. 148–160.

Raspotnik, A., Jacob, M. and Ventura, L., 2012. *Discussion Paper: The Issue of Solidarity in the European Union.* [Online] Available at: http://www.tepsa.eu/download/TEPSA%20Discussion%20Paper%20The%20issue%20of%20solidarity %20in%20the%20European%20Union.pdf [Accessed 21 March 2021].

Rea, A., Martiniello, M., Mazzola, A. and Meuleman, B., 2019. *The Refugee Reception Crisis in Europe Polarized Opinions and Mobilizations.* Bruxelles: l'Université de Bruxelles.

The Council of Refugee Women in Bulgaria, n.d. *The Council of Refugee Women in Bulgaria.* [Online] Available at: https://crw-bg.org/en/direct-work-programs [Accessed 5 April 2021].

Todorov, A., 2009. Y a-t-il démocratie sans participation?. In: A. Krasteva, ed. *Engagement citoyen.* Sofia: NBU, pp. 16–28.

Todorov, T., 2017. *Nepokorni [Insoumis].* Sofia: s.n.

UNHCR, 2016. *UNHCR in Bulgaria.* [Online] Available at: https://www.unhcr.org/bg/142-bgza-nasvkboon-v-blgariya-html.html [Accessed 20 March 2021].

Vankova, Z., Ilareva, V. and Bechev, D., 2017. Bulgaria, the EU and the 'Refugee Crisis. How to Improve the Policies on International Protection and Refugee Integration?. [Online] Available at: http://eupolicy.eu/wp-content/uploads/2017/04/doklad_bejanci_final.pdf

Wagner, M., Kraler, A. and Baumgartner, P., 2018. *Solidarity – An Integral and Basic Concept of the Common European Asylum System.* s.l.: CEASEVAL project.

Conclusion
Bulgaria's lessons, European tendencies

"The long summer of migration" has drastically affected European societies. Migration, which can be capitalised upon as a demographic, intellectual, and cultural potential, was instrumentalised in a demonising fashion by the populist wave, which has swept over Europe – as a menace and as a burden. Bulgarian specifics provide an interesting field, affording opportunities for wider theoretical interpretations.

The short migration history and the ongoing transit character of the migratory flows have clearly outlined the tendency of populist discourses to engender societal notions transcending the data-based realities. The construction of symbolic universes by a wide range of political actors has been used to substitute real problems of society by way of conjuring up enemies "inside" or "outside" (Wodak, 2015, p. 51) – whether asylum-seeking migrants, traditional minorities, sexual minorities, or even international documents such as the Istanbul Convention. These Bulgarian lessons provide a good reference point for analysis of both European and global tendencies.

Since the turn of the twenty-first century, radical politics have entered a new phase. While populism is not a new phenomenon and has existed historically across a number of regions, populist political actors and parties have risen significantly in recent years across almost all regions of the world. Electoral successes of populist politicians and parties in the past decade have posed challenges to both established and younger democracies (International IDEA, 2020). Over the past decades, populist and radical actors have mobilised through electoral and protest channels and succeeded in radicalising 'mainstream' politics on the European continent and beyond. Numbers of research address the reasons which led to the spread of this phenomenon that challenged the stability of the democracy. The analysis of the Bulgarian case allowed us to propose three main factors that could explain the origins of the described populist wave. Those are (1) the democratic

DOI: 10.4324/9781003161493-7

deficit; (2) the overlapping crises over crises; and (3) the digitalisation of the public sphere.

The combination of these three factors proved a powerful catalyst for what we have called in our text "normalization" of populism. Normalisation occurs on several levels.

The first is through the process of imposing of topics while populist and radical parties have been responsible for the politicisation of a number of issues (environmentalism, immigration, Euroscepticism, etc.), the issues at the core of their ideology are no longer exclusively owned by these organisations. Indeed, they have profoundly reshaped social and political cleavages at the national and supranational level (Gattinara, 2020).

The second – through reinforcing the role of the discourse. The narrative about policies becomes more important than policies themselves. Verbalising the crisis rather than numbers is responsible to a much greater extent for creating the crisis. The talk about migration is more important than policymaking in the field of migration. Ruth Wodak talks about a process of fictionalisation of politics

> that is, "the blurring of boundaries in politics between the real and the fictional, the informative and the entertaining" that creates a reality for the viewer which appears ordered and manageable – and thus presents a deceptively simple illusion in contrast to the very real complexity and pluralism of present-day societies.
>
> (Wodak, 2015, p. 34)

In a situation where the right-wing parties get an easy access to media democracy (Wodak, 2015), the competition of political actors shifts to a different field and we observe precisely this process of normalisation of extreme and until recently unacceptable language. This is another reason to have preference for the term "populism" in this analysis. The way of doing politics, enacted by the far-right parties, is equally valid for everyone infected with it, especially when it comes to sensible issues like migration. It is precisely within this line of reasoning that the symbolic dimension of 'doing politics' should be thought of (Wodak, 2015). Rydgren writes:

> For the radical right, immigrants are a threat to ethno-national identity; second, they are a major cause of criminality and other kinds of social insecurity; third, they are a cause of unemployment; and fourth, they are abusers of the generosity of the welfare states of Western democracies, which results in fewer state subsidies, etc., for natives.
>
> (Rydgren, 2007, p. 242)

In the preceding pages, however, we have repeatedly seen this argumentation in the talk of actors from the entire political spectrum.

For a long time in Bulgaria, "classic" populist parties in the country, mostly from the patriotic and the populist spectrum had marginal significance in political life and comparatively peripheral electoral support. The presence of such parties was evaluated more as a phenomenon with eccentric nuance rather than a rule. If we can show two major moments where the different populist waves emerge, they relate mostly to the exhaustion of the post-1989 transition cleavage and the second, with the exhaustion of the classic right-left cleavage and mostly with the voidance of the right-left spectrum parties from ideological content, has opened favourable space in the poorest European country for the national-populist discourse to gain popularity. In the previous chapters, however, we have explained why this does not imply that populism in Bulgaria is leftist as in the understanding of researchers such as Chantal Mouffe (Mouffe, 2018) or Giovanna Campani (Campani, 2019). The democratic deficits, the withdrawal of citizens from the political, valid both in the national context and when it comes to the EU political system, is a cause for alarm in established democracies and those in transition alike. This widening of the distance between citizens and rulers is actually one of the most winning populist strategies, now classic, of contraposition of people to elite. The crisis in the political is being intensified by the modern world's unique characteristic associated with overlapping crisis periods. Modern societies are faced with the challenge of living in a crisis – financial, migrational, ecological, and medical. This instability actuates civil discontent, which usually finds manifestations in frequent protests, moods for a change in the model of government, which again is being adroitly instrumentalised by populism. In this sense, Ruth Wodak reminds:

As argued by Murray Edelman in his seminal book The Symbolic Uses of Politics (1967), crises are promoted to serve the interests of political leaders and other interest groups who will most certainly benefit from such definitions (e.g. Altheide, 2002, p. 12).

(Wodak, 2015, p. 27)

Its characteristic is the capture of the civil mood and the gratification, primarily at discursive level, of the expectations of criticism and change. As we have pointed out, populists tend to engage more in talking and less – in making policies. This is especially visible in the Bulgarian case where, precisely in periods of crises, policies are discontinued.

The third level of normalisation occurs through the promotion of parties from the far-right spectrum to the rank of coalition partners. The conspicuous absence of a cordon sanitaire in the political life of Bulgaria has ensured a new forum for their expression. There was an expectation that the extreme parties would be tamed but reality showed that the entire political terrain was altered. In addition to vivid media presence, parliamentary forum not just legitimised their presence and intensified the effect of the topics and discourses imposed by them, but also voided the institutions of credence and content. There are three areas which can be identified in this respect: agenda-setting power and deflection, euphemisation and trivialisation, and amplification (Brown and Mondon, 2020). This is most apparent in the (non)implemented public policies of the government. We cannot help agreeing with Cas Mudde that

> In fact, mainstream rightwing parties are more responsible for the recent anti-immigration turn than populist radical right parties. While all have moved to a more strict immigration and integration position, some have chosen to use this particular issue to gain governmental power by co-opting either the populist radical right parties or their voters. In most of these cases, the mainstream right adopted not just a more radical immigration position, but also implemented more strict immigration policies than in other countries.
>
> (Mudde, 2016, p. 14)

This is why we have repeatedly emphasised that not so much the genesis of these parties is alarming, as the "embrace" of populism on the part of the mainstream parties. In a situation of strong distrust for institutions, politicians, and the political process as a whole, one can only respond to populism with more populism.

What serves as a fresh fuel and is bound to have increasing importance is the digitalisation of the public sphere and politics. We witness strong fragmentation and polarisation of the public sphere, different models of formation of the public opinion and new channels of political communication. These specifics, which in a different perspective would have a revitalising effect on democracy, are precisely among the reasons for the flourishing of a new type of populism – "digital populism". Digital populism not only uses digital platforms to allow politicians to communicate with the electorate, but also bases its political programme directly in the power of social media and its potential for manipulation (Zabala, 2020). In a world dominated by post-truth and fake news, populists are bound to win and the process of normalisation of populism is bound to intensify. As we have described in our text, the first populist parties in Bulgaria have also gathered strength through television channels and newspapers of their own. What changes with digitisation, however, is the scale, the speed, the price and the effect of the message. It should be noted that the usage of artificial intellect for the purposes of marketing targeting of electorate is also a unique phenomenon relating to the success of the populists. This is the reason for a distinction to be drawn in our text between analogue and digital populists, which have made their appearance in Bulgarian political stage in the recent years.

The examples of solidarity and civil activity, depicted in the book, which we have seen as a natural antidote of populist displays, are actually possible and happen precisely on account of the same factors, which are responsible for the floruit of populism. The disillusionment with the political, the crisis situations, as well as the digital world tend to stimulate and even facilitate the most positive examples of responding to the migration crisis. Moreover, in the text we share the understanding that acts of citizenship of informed and empowered citizens can change the dominating attitudes, narratives and logical frameworks of the power in order to transform society and politics.

Bibliography

Altheide, D. L., 2002. *Creating Fear: News and the Construction of Crisis.* New York: Transaction.

Brown, K., and Mondon, A., 2020. Populism, the media, and the mainstreaming of the far right: The Guardian's coverage of populism as a case study. *Politics*, 41(3), pp. 279–295.

Campani, G., 2019. The migration crisis between populism and post-democracy. In: G. Fitzi, J. Mackert and Bryan S. Turner, eds. *Populism and the Crisis of Democracy Volume 3: Migration, Gender and Religion.* London: Routledge, pp. 29–47.

Gattinara, P. C., 2020. *Populism, Radicalism and Extremism: At the Margins and into the Mainstream.* [Online] Available at: https://ecpr.eu/Events/Event/SectionDetails/911 [Accessed 6 April 2021].

International IDEA, 2020. Populist government and democracy: An impact assessment using the Global State of Democracy Indices. *GSoD In Focus*, February 14.

Mouffe, C., 2018. *For a Left Populism.* London: Verso.

Mudde, C., 2016. *On Extremism and Democracy in Europe.* London: Routledge.

Rydgren, J., 2007. The sociology of the radical right. *Annual Review of Sociology*, 33, pp. 241–262.

Wodak, R., 2015. *The Politics of Fear.* SAGE Publications Ltd.

Zabala, S., 2020. Beware of digital populism. *Aljazeera.* February 7. [Online] Available at: https://www.aljazeera.com/opinions/2020/2/7/beware-of-digital-populism [Accessed 21 May 2021].

Index

anti-elitist 89, 95, 118
anti-immigration 49, 132
anti-systemic 87, 89, 95, 99
asylum seekers 2, 7, 27, 50, 51, 68, 72, 73, 74, 75, 76, 77, 78, 81, 99, 114, 115, 118, 119, 123, 124
Ataka 58, 63, 88, 89, 92, 93, 94, 96, 98, 105, 117

Balkan Refugee Route 3, 4, 7, 22, 41, 49, 50, 61, 67, 74, 84
border 2, 3, 4, 7, 8, 16, 26, 38, 41, 42, 43, 50, 51, 53, 54, 55, 58, 59, 60, 61, 75, 78, 80, 97, 99, 112, 116, 123, 126
Borisov, B. 57, 88, 91, 94, 97, 117
BSP 53, 54, 55, 58, 93, 94, 95, 96, 99, 104, 105, 117, 118
Bulgarian citizenship 17, 39, 45, 46, 47, 71
Bulgarian Council on Refugees and Migrants–BCRM 116
Bulgarian Helsinki Committee 43, 75, 79, 80, 124
Bulgarian origin 39, 46, 47, 48, 68
Bulgarian Red Cross 122, 123
Bulgarian Socialist Party 50, 57, 104

campaigns 24, 25, 49, 50, 52, 113, 123, 124
Caritas 23
citizenship 2, 10, 13, 15, 16, 17, 39, 45, 46, 47, 48, 71, 108, 120, 121, 122, 126, 133
civic structures 112

civil activity 7, 113, 133
civil networks 112
Common European Asylum System (CEAS) 5, 57, 69, 117
communist 1, 4, 8, 9, 10, 23, 37, 87, 90, 100, 119, 120, 121
communities 7, 8, 19, 21, 22, 53, 61, 75, 80, 115, 119, 121, 122, 126
corruption 15, 41, 47, 50, 51, 89, 90, 95, 97, 101
Covid-19 pandemic 16, 17, 44

discourse 23, 28, 37, 42, 45, 49, 50, 52, 55, 56, 57, 61, 68, 80, 81, 91, 93, 95, 98, 99, 101, 103, 118, 119, 125, 129, 130, 131, 132

elections 47, 52, 59, 71, 87, 88, 90, 94, 96, 97
elite 26, 88, 95, 99, 100, 101, 102, 103, 113, 118, 131
ethnicity 40, 43, 77
EU citizenship 47
European legislation 67, 70, 115
Europeanisation 5, 90, 116, 117
Euroscepticism 85, 90, 118, 130
exclusion 45, 81, 125
extremist parties 4, 50, 85, 87, 91, 92

fake news 52, 54, 97, 133
far-right 3, 5, 53, 56, 84, 91, 100, 121, 126, 130, 132
feminisation of migrations 12
foreign citizens 39, 48
Friends of the Refugees 119, 124

For Product Safety Concerns and Information please contact our EU
representative GPSR@taylorandfrancis.com
Taylor & Francis Verlag GmbH, Kaufingerstraße 24, 80331 München, Germany